off the leash

off the leash
a year at the dog park

matthew gilbert

Thomas Dunne Books • St. Martin's Griffin • New York

For Tom, and for Toby
My caravan

THOMAS DUNNE BOOKS.
An imprint of St. Martin's Press.

www.thomasdunnebooks.com
www.stmartins.com

The Library of Congress has cataloged the hardcover edition as follows:

Gilbert, Matthew, 1958–
    Off the leash : a year at the dog park / Matthew Gilbert. — First edition.
        p. cm.
    "Thomas Dunne Books."
    ISBN 978-1-250-01422-1 (hardcover)
    ISBN 978-1-250-01421-4 (e-book)
    1. Dogs—Behavior—Anecdotes. 2. Parks for dogs—Anecdotes. I. Title.
    SF433.G55 2014
    636.7'089689142—dc23

                                                                    2014008424

ISBN 978-1-250-01457-3 (trade paperback)

Our books may be purchased in bulk for promotional, educational, or business use. Please contact your local bookseller or the Macmillan Corporate and Premium Sales Department at 1-800-221-7945, extension 5442, or by e-mail at MacmillanSpecialMarkets@macmillan.com.

First St. Martin's Griffin Edition: April 2016

10 9 8 7 6 5 4 3 2 1

Amory dog park remains a safe haven for dog owners and dogs, a place that, ideally, is free of self-consciousness and judgment. And so, to preserve the inviolability of that sweet state, I have disguised the people and the dogs and created composites. I have changed names, facial features, hair color, snout sizes, and breeds. I have also altered chronology to form a dog park mash-up, a re-creation of a year. I hope Amory people recognize the characteristics I portray but none of the characters.

contents

a cast of characters

Hayley, With the Brave Armor
Stewie, the Burnese Mountain Role Model

Nash, Who Pitches Irony
Bertha the Golden Love Bucket

Margo, Mother of Us All
Travis, Lord of all Balls

Ky, Stoner Poet and Poop Strewer
Trixie, She of the Raw Diet

Drew the Guy
Chester, Ridgeback Mix and Loyal Bro

Not-Sweet Charlotte
Sugar, a Whippet With Ribs and Teeth

Cell Phone Lady, Her Shoulder to the Wind
The Westie Misses Hope and Midge

OTHERS:
Officer Marvelous
Saul the walker
Noreen, who talks TV

Me: One of them.

I like to read books on dog training. . . . Every sentence is a riot.

—E. B. White

You can discover more about a person in an hour of play than in a year of conversation.

—Plato

introduction

Even though it's morning, the sun is giving everything—the browning hillside, the faces and jackets of the dog owners, Toby's waggling blond body—a thick golden late-afternoon tint. It's fall, and I'm standing with a group of people in the great field at the local dog park, Amory, watching our city dogs run off-leash. Fallen orange and yellow leaves are getting kicked up by four or five of the dogs as they chase a swift Italian greyhound named Enzo en masse, none quite reaching him, none truly wanting to reach him and end the game. Enzo sprints forward like a flung rubber band, his limbs loose, all effortless thrust; the other dogs are his biggest fans, his paparazzi.

I'm laughing out loud because Toby, my one-and-a-half-year-old preteen yellow Lab, has tagged on at the very back of the careening pack. He's not built for speed, and on some level he seems to know it. He's actually running in an inner circle of the pack's circle, the wheel within the wheel, almost ready to cut across the middle to try to catch the It dog. Technically, he's just run-walking, his jaw slack, his soft brown eyes hypnotized by the prize, Enzo.

Toby's chunky face is so earnest, so fixed on the amazing Enzo and his legions, so obviously dazzled by the possibility of being the one to catch him that I am madly in love with him at this moment. His transparency is contagious, and I say, "Look at that goose" to the stranger standing next to me, not caring what he thinks. Just saying the word *goose* out loud feels luxurious. I feel a little like a parent, kvelling over how adorable my child is, like Mrs. Berger from my hometown, who always bragged—even to children—about how lucky she was because she had "three wonderful kids." She'd say it like "thray wundaful kidsss." So I'm a shamelessly proud dog parent today. But mostly, I feel like a child, a happy boy cheering out loud about a game at the playground, unconstrained by my adult hang-ups and inhibitions, which are intricate and would have made Mrs. Berger plotz in her midi skirts and patent-leather boots.

All of a sudden, across the Amory field, a vision: Toby spots a gauzy, glittering dreamboat moving from the park entrance onto the grass, like a Hollywood starlet stepping out of a limo and onto the red carpet. He promptly drops off of the Enzo train, instantly forgetting the big chase in order to stare at his beloved Nellie, who is now jogging toward the crowd with her owner trailing behind her, her long legs in a moderate gallop.

Nellie is a tall fawn Great Dane, and she looms large in Toby's universe as the dog who will always gladly chase him around Amory, from the middle of the field, where dog owners often stand—it's the overlapping outfields of two baseball diamonds—to the bordering hillside and back. She is Toby's latest sweetheart. Most of the park dogs, like most of the people I know, prefer to be chased after; dog behavior and human behavior aren't as different as the dog manuals might have it. There are dogs and people who must dominate every group they're in, dogs and people who lash out because they're fearful, and, yes, dogs and people who very much prefer to be the object of desire—the chased—rather than "the more loving one" that the poet W. H. Auden wrote about. But Nellie the giant, she just loves to gallop after Toby with her lanky legs cantering and her hanging jowls jiggling. She is a committed Toby chaser. And she never seems able to catch him, despite the length of her stride and the intensity of her aspiration. She trails behind and above him like a gigantic Disney balloon at the Macy's Thanksgiving Day Parade.

In an instant, Toby snatches up a dirty tennis ball left on the patchy grass and tears ass, and Nellie, with her sad, wise eyes and her black mask, falls in behind him as they enact their ritual. They've known each other for months, and they've gotten their game down pat. They run in wide-open circles. I walk over to Nellie's owner, Lucinda, and we laugh together as we watch them in the golden light. We've seen this routine more than a dozen times, and it still pleases us.

"*And now it's Toby dog in the lead, with Nellie's dog close behind*," Lucinda says in the voice of a sports announcer, holding her fist up to her mouth as if it's a microphone. "*Toby's running for his life, but what's this? The great Nellie is catching up, having tired out her competitor.*"

She holds the "mike" up to me. "It's Scooby-Doo running after Brian from *Family Guy*," I announce, making an analogy to the TV cartoon Great Dane and the TV cartoon yellow

Lab—because everything in life somehow comes back to TV, right? I was a child of TV, I am the TV critic for the *Boston Globe*, and my thinking process is automatically wired to compare the world out there to the world on-screen. Every living thing, it seems, has some parallel to Saturday-morning TV or *The Twilight Zone* or *Seinfeld*. I've got IMDb for brains.

But Lucinda, with thick purple-tinted glasses and close-cropped brown hair, looks at me with a tilted head and a squinched up "Huh—what?" face, and I laugh some more and clap my hands. I feel playful out here on the Amory grass, yelling about a cartoon chase that sounds like pure nonsense to her, openly smitten with Toby and his little victory, unashamed of my lifelong inability to tell a joke. As with the dogs at Amory, improvising joy at our feet, dancing like Snoopy did on his doghouse under the stars, circling in a chase for the sake of a chase, my pleasure is unedited.

For most of my life, I was the last person on earth you'd have expected to find malingering at a dog park, laughing openly like a fool with a muddy leash around my shoulders and with broken biscuits and poop bags in my pockets. I was that guy who rolled his eyes at people who treat their dogs like children. Dogs were dirty and scary, I felt, and I would cross the street or charge forward when faced with a person leading his or her dog on the sidewalk. I wasn't Cruella de Vil, but all my thoughts regarding dogs and dog people ranged from negative to indifferent.

But I fell in love with a dog person, and then I fell in love with dogs. And in the year plus since my husband, Tom, and I got the seven-week-old Toby from a New Hampshire breeder and he began pulling me to Amory, I've fallen in love with the dog park. I have changed, let go of so much baggage, opened myself up to the eccentric ways of dog communities. I still have moments of cynicism and fear and judgment, like just about every good person I know in this world; reports of the existence of pure unending happiness and acceptance and compassion are greatly exaggerated. But now I have a guaranteed daily chance to feel a part of something live and kicking. Over the past year, I've undergone a shakedown by a chaotic puppy regarding my control issues; I've become part of a loose community of weirdly wonderful dog people—a pack of freaks; and, on a deeper level, I've shed my hyperawareness of the inevitability of loss. Shadowed by the death of my father when I was three, by the emotional knowledge of where this all goes sooner or later, I finally got dragged into the lighter, more light-filled world of dogs and the people who accompany them. Dogs, those gusts of spirit, bring us into our own hearts, but they are also a bridge to other people.

It's a cliché; I totally know that—dogs as saviors, dog people as lovably crazy. And yet there it is, my truth and the truth of many of the dog owners I've gotten to know so well from the park. We watch the dogs run free and feel their freedom. The nakedness of their desires amuses and inspires us. They get us out of bed and to the park on brain-clouded mornings. They are little gusts of spirit that can transform us, put us on tack.

Sometimes you're not a cliché, but sometimes, it turns out, you are.

Amory came into our lives when Toby was about three months old. The little guy clearly needed to get out of our third-floor Brookline walk-up and run—a lot. He was scrambling, from the den couch to under my desk and into the radiator covers, with his oversized paws slipping and sliding on the hardwood floor.

I would have preferred to stay one-on-one and two-on-one with him, finding places to take him and Tom on nature walks, since urban sidewalks can be trafficky. I had an old-fashioned image of a boy and his loyal dog somewhere in the back of my mind, and so did Tom. Newly married—our ceremony was one month after gay marriage became legal in Massachusetts in 2004—we fantasized about having this alternative nuclear family, with Toby running ahead of us as we hiked through the wilderness, looking back at us as he led us forward. Two boys and their dog, a tacit and protective union, free of the grown-up world—maybe there were singing butterflies buzzing around us in that picture. . . .

But Toby was having none of that. It wasn't that he tormented Tom and me about getting out and mingling; but once he was outside and near other dogs, he was so crazy with happiness and ready to throw himself around, we couldn't resist giving him that experience. He'd tear ass in circles whenever he was in an open field with playmates, a yellow whirlwind, his silky ears dancing up from his head. It was deeply satisfying to watch him find his footing.

Amory is only seven or eight blocks from our apartment, right by the Boston-Brookline border, a pastoral few acres with two flat, open baseball fields. Bordered on one side by a tree-filled slope down from Amory Street and on the other with a row of weeping willows sheltering a few picnic tables, it is tucked deep into the moderately busy neighborhood. You can walk by Amory without quite realizing you're on the edge of a little pastoral haven. If you're a distracted Boston University student in flip-flops, or a nine-to-five carpooler heading to downtown Boston, or a local pizza shop owner, or me about a year ago, you probably buzz by the park a few times a day without thinking twice. But if you are a Frisbee player, or a jogger, or a new mom with a carriage, or a dog owner, or a dog, you probably know the park inside out, from its stinky green plastic garbage cans to the textures of its spongy, sometimes muddy turf. Sometimes when neighborhood dogs get loose and run off, the owners find them at Amory, their second home.

Those first weeks when I started taking Toby to Amory, I felt like an outsider among the chance groupings of dog people; it was my default social position. I automatically retreated to the periphery. Plus, what little I'd heard and seen during my visits was not tempting. At a glance, dog people can seem like a thorny crew. There was something about full-on dog play, with its attendant dogfights, that seemed to amplify the human interaction nearby; it was like everyone had downed a few cans of Red Bull. Dogs in groups can create an atmosphere of extroversion and expressiveness among the owners, and that isn't always pretty. "Get a handle on your damned dog, man," I heard a young guy with a beagle yell at a bent-over elderly dog owner early on, his voice dripping with contempt. Like the dogs, the people at the park sometimes broke their training, slipped the hold of civilization, dropped their adult masks, and became emotional children throwing sand in the sandbox.

During my initial visits, I overheard angry complaints about how this one never stops talking, and talking loudly, and how that one doesn't have enough control over her dogs. Poop—he doesn't pick his up; she doesn't pick all of hers up. I heard hostile chatter about Officer Marv, a cop who liked to harass dog owners. People would say "Marv" with ironic affect, sinking their teeth into the name. When I got a load of said Marv, a runty fellow who looked like a pint-size Archie Bunker with a badge, I felt instant acrimony from him and toward him as he brusquely checked Toby for his registration tag. At first, the dog park seemed kind of tense.

And truly, it is a strangely random—and, with the ballooning number of dog owners in the United States, a growing— subculture. These were people who would not normally intermingle—some of whom were on the social fringes and would not usually blend with other people at all—except that their dogs had insisted on it. All that the dog park people definitely had in common were feelings for dogs and a commitment to letting their dogs have time to be with other dogs. They were thrown-togethers, like the cast of *Gilligan's Island*, group therapy members, or *Canterbury Tales* pilgrims, and so there could be raw psychodynamics and huge cultural gulfs, on top of the spats about the subcultural rules and rituals involving dog toys and dog poop and humping. It was a microcosm, a compact and somewhat peeled-back version of the social world at large, with its conflicts and ganging up and partisan splits. And there were fewer places to hide at the park than there were out there, and less insulation, as the colliding dogs forced interaction among strangers.

But Toby needed to be among his kind, and he pulled me into the park, unable to understand or care that I'd rather sit at home stopping time, lost in staring at him while he wrestled with a stuffed hedgehog on his back, using his big yellow paws like hands, or while he slept, his eyelids closed but blinking. He was innocent and hungry to play and always at the ready for what writer Tony Kushner boiled down to an essence in *Angels in America*: "More life."

And eventually, as the months of my first year passed, I also became fully engaged in the dog park, just as much as Toby. Toby would cry with excitement and pace in the backseat of the car when we'd pull into the Amory parking lot, his tail like a bongo player against the fabric, and I began to feel that same anticipation. I became smitten with the place, with the people, with the commotion, with the pack energy. And I became fascinated by the liberating effect that dog play can have on the people watching it.

This book isn't about an instant life transformation thanks to a dog so much as it's about those great daily tugs of the leash, how visits to a place can accumulate into an adventure, how Toby gradually drew me into a more spontaneous and playful state of mind, where the specter of loss no longer served as my guide. It's a portrait of savoring ordinary life. Ultimately, I would let go of Toby's leash at the park, and *I'd* let go. Some people find their daily Zen in meditation, or in jogging, or in playing guitar. Many, like Tom, feel the invitation to love alone with a dog. That first year of Toby's life, I found my way into the moments of my own life in the mundane improvisations of the park universe, with golden days of dogs playing and jumping on my feet, with unplanned meetings with new friends and weird strangers, with impromptu beers and the kind of loyalty that comes with surviving dog illnesses and dogfights and people fights, too.

It was a sweet evolution, a falling up, the way Toby and I found a park rhythm that year.

fall

backstories

We all land at Amory with backstories, with our particular situations, needs, and histories, and we all find something there, beyond the practicalities of getting our dogs out of the house and off the sidewalk. It's just a dog park, but dog parks have come to occupy a special position in modern life, as an ad hoc institution built on play, proximity, and pack relationships. We all have to interact there; our dogs make it happen. We don't have the protections of a PTA-like organization or the rules of sports games or the separations afforded by our cell phones; the dogs break through the padding of technology, force contact. We end up creating the tone of the outdoor community with one another on a daily basis.

For me, the park was a megadose of presence. I was a full-on TV junkie, beginning as a kid who took his serial story lines and TV events very seriously. I remember grieving for days when Col. Henry Blake died on *M*A*S*H,* laughing out loud when Kimberly removed her wig to reveal she was a scarred madwoman on *Melrose Place,* and feeling scandalized when Sinéad O'Connor tore up a picture of the Pope on *Saturday*

Night Live. I was four, I was eight, I was fifteen, I was sixteen, I was twenty-three, and I was forty-two and working happily as TV critic for the *Boston Globe,* and TV was my consistent and close companion. Throughout those decades, I embraced the state of electronic thrall, that pleasing equation of being there plus not being there.

Sitting on this side of the glass, I fell in love for the first time when I was nine, in the den of our southeastern Massachusetts home. My father was long gone, that indistinct furniture sales-man who'd left me with one vague memory—of his lifting me up to sit on a wooden desk, the lamp giving his hands a golden cast. I was watching black-and-white repeats of *The Dick Van Dyke Show* every day on TV, and secretly adopting Rob Petrie as my real dad. He was a goofy string bean of a man, an urban comedy writer with a suburban family. I loved him at age nine for his stumbles and social gaffes, for his macho-free masculin-ity, for the rare birds in his life, like his cowriters, Buddy and Sally, and I still do decades later. Those half hours with Rob Petrie had a religious character for me. I became one with the TV screen—knees on the floor, elbows on a footstool facing the set, hand on chin.

You've been there, no doubt, fed by the dependable love of the remote-controlled breast. You've visited that place of com-fortable numbness, where the world is like another TV show. It's not a bad place. I lived there for years at a time, through high school and college and my twenties, perfectly content to have a screen between me and other people. I made a very sat-isfying career out of it. Watching TV for the *Globe,* I scribbled down endless notes, thinking about the American character as I watched the boyish Dexter kill killers or the CSIs pick through the fetishes of Las Vegas. I became well versed in the existential fears of *The Twilight Zone* and the global paranoia of *Lost,* and when I stumbled across a new TV classic, a *Mad Men* or an *Arrested Development,* I felt high.

Sometimes, my husband, Tom, would be my TV copilot, sitting beside me in flight. He'd generously become my partner on the couch, celebrating when the networks sent advance episodes of the great shows and suffering through a portion of the junk pile—the shrill, idiotic sitcoms and generic cop dramas that every TV critic must sample. A political affairs guy by nature and profession, Tom nonetheless submitted to about a fourth of my viewing time (except when it came to reality TV, regarding which he told me I was on my own). And over the years, as the professional TV guy, I'd developed elaborate viewing rituals that Tom had come to tolerate. My viewing time was sacred. He knew I needed to sit with the screen in the exact center of my field of vision. He knew I didn't like to answer the phone or look at the caller ID during a good show. And he knew no one in the room should talk unless the episode had been put on pause.

Toby, however, could not be put on pause. No TV, he.

Tom and I brought Toby home in early October of 2004, a seven-week-old yellow Lab reaction ball of crazy love with baby teeth like carpet tacks. He was just perfect, with his Buddha belly, which felt like a firm down pillow. His energized little dashes and tumbles fell somewhere between acrobatics and expert slapstick comedy. Human beings practice for years to do what Toby was doing before he was even toilet-trained.

He felt like a miracle to me, from top to bottom, with his daily growth spurts, his already giant paws, the softness of his ears, and his dead-on stare up at us after he dropped a toy or a stick at our feet. From the moment we got him home, I couldn't stop contemplating his flawlessness. I'd say to myself, "I have a dog named Toby," as if it were some kind of incantation.

He instantly changed the layout of our third-floor Brookline walk-up—and of our settled, professionally centered lives. We baby-gated the kitchen, and we turned the space under the small square kitchen table into a fort for one of his crates. Another crate—yes, Toby's two daddies overdid it on the crate business—took over our small bedroom. We raised all our ground-level plants, and we put musty old carpets down on our slippery wood floors so the little guy could get his footing. Tom and I stopped sleeping for a few weeks, and we both took vacation time to make sure one of us was always with him. It was not uncommon to look away and look back at a shredded document on the floor, or a pool of pee with paw prints trailing off it.

To find my first dog, I had spent months asking friends for breeder contacts and looking online at hundreds of breeder Web sites, gawking at their photos, succumbing to their cheesy Hallmark music. I was thinking that I could somehow design my future dog's personality by choosing carefully. Ultimately, I landed on Mirabelle Labs, whose site was jammed with photos and dog family trees. I loved the look of the Mirabelle stock—mid-size, a little square-headed—and reached out to owner Dana Loud, who, after reading my application to buy one of her planned puppies, welcomed Tom and me for a visit to see her farm. Apparently, she wasn't scared off by my too-personal answers to her basic questions about food brands and dog safety; I'd written out a lengthy worrywart debate with myself about whether or not it's okay to let a dog ride in a car with his head out the window, since there would be cars and trucks passing by. I guess she could tell that, beyond my neurosis, or because I needed to channel it productively, Tom and I were looking to take special care of a Toby.

Visiting Dana's farm that spring, we met a black Lab named Mia, who, if all went according to plan and her encounter with a yellow named Drake was a success, would be the mother of our puppy. Mia was a bouncy lady who was delighted to see us, loping in circles around us as Tom and I laughed at her. Dana told us she bred for friendliness, and it was obvious she was pulling it off. Mia was one of those dogs—Toby is, too—who really do seem to smile at you. She smiled at us and wiggled her torso and jogged, her mostly furless belly a tad distended from previous litters, her nipples quite visible. She was irresistibly welcoming.

"This will be her last litter," Dana told us as we sat in her yard, making it all seem so much dearer.

Tom and I felt very close during this period, just having gotten married and now preparing for our new family member. A lot of couples see puppies as rehearsals for babies; we saw our puppy as an end in himself, a cementing of our home life together. Neither one of us wanted children, a fact we'd established early in our relationship. But we wanted mutual responsibility; we wanted to share our apartment and our love with another creature.

We returned to Dana's farm five weeks after Mia had given birth, in September, to choose from the two yellows in her litter of six. I'd told Tom I wanted to get the whitest of the yellows, because I loved fluffy whiteness, and indeed one of the two was a milky little fellow. But his slightly darker brother stole our hearts, with his strangely knowing glance, an expression Toby still gets when he's lazily looking our way from his comfortable couch or bed. He gazes out beneficently on the people. Inside the pen on Dana's thick New Hampshire grass, turning his head with its outsize snout to look straight at us while his fellow puppies slept and wrestled around him, little Toby, with his teasing eyes, said, "I'd sure like to chase you two fellas around a dining room table—you know you want to." He seemed to be quietly plotting ways to find a ball, drop it at our feet, and make us throw it. Physically, he was just this side of a guinea pig at five weeks, but he already seemed to have a fully defined personality built on jokey roguishness. He lay there staring at us on the late-summer grass, fenced in with his siblings and another litter, this one consisting of six chocolate Labs, and Tom and I were gonesville.

In the car, I quickly said, "I loved the yellower puppy," and Tom sighed.

"Phew. Me, too."

When we picked up Toby from Dana two weeks later, we had a small crate in the backseat—yes, another crate—and we put him inside for the two-and-a-half-hour ride back to Boston. We didn't want him jumping and peeing all over the car, or getting thrown around by turns. It was his first time in a crate and in a car, and Toby began crying out immediately, making the first part of the ride, through some gorgeous early-fall New England landscapes, miserable. I couldn't bear his helpless wailing, which continued until he fell asleep after twenty or so endless minutes. I was sure we were scarring him for life. They weren't like baby cries, those alarming jolts; to my sensitive ears, they seemed to be imbued with sadness. We were traumatizing the joy out of him. We were tearing him away from his mother. I sat in the backseat, next to the crate, fretting, while Tom, who'd had dogs almost all his life, sat at the wheel, secretly rolling his eyes at my hypersensitivity. He understood a dog's resilience far better than I.

Once home, our car ride was a distant memory for Toby—more likely, not even a memory. Toby instantly tore around the kitchen like a tiny blond tornado while we entertained him for fifteen minutes, a pattern that took hold. That first October that we had him, before the park was on the agenda, we all seemed to operate in fifteen-minute-long sessions. He'd be the feisty ringleader for that period. He'd pick up stuffed toys in his mouth without quite knowing what to do with them, swatting the air with his giant paws, running and looking back to make sure we were chasing him; and then—bam—asleep, on the spot.

As Toby would lie snoozing, I'd lie on my side next to him on the tile floor, staring at his perfect snout, examining its delicate geometric system of whiskers, watching his moist black nostrils flex so slightly, his eyelids flinch in dream state, his heart putter beneath his fur. I felt as though I could stare for hours, dazzled by his happy innocence, his complete unselfconsciousness, his lack of impulse control. It was parenting, albeit in a different way. Knowing that he'd wake up and see my face looming over him, and not be frightened—it touched me. I'd put my nose up to his belly, sniff, and smell something irresistible—warm popcorn, maybe, or fresh promise. I felt like

I could do this forever. Tom would catch me and laugh, thinking of how long I'd resisted getting a dog. I was lying on the dirty floor, for one thing, and I was in a stupor of adoration. He saw me falling in love with Toby, and I saw him falling in love with Toby, and it was so peaceful.

Lying there, looking at the puppy sleeping after a round of play, detached from my remote control, I already sensed that he had some kind of curative power over me, that he could somehow wake me up. This gorgeous blob of chaos was going to dominate me.

At that time, I became obsessed with training. The assault on our daily routines was lovely, but it also sent me into recovery mode. We contacted a local guy who advertised online for home dog training and made an appointment. Don, in his twenties, with a brown shag haircut, came to our house one bright October morning, and in that hour, he told us that being firm and direct with your dog was the key to mastering him. As it turned out, we needed training, not Toby, and particularly me. After talking about how dogs want leadership, he took us down to the sidewalk for a walking session, pulling Toby forward despite Toby's efforts to sniff at trees and jump up at his legs. He told us that Toby's neck was strong, so we shouldn't worry about tugging on the leash for correction.

"Always keeps him on the same side behind you as you walk," Don explained.

"If he runs ahead of you and tries to be the leader, stop and stand in place to show him who's boss," Don advised.

"Always make him sit before you take off his leash," Don recommended.

When Don used our dog's name he said "*TOBY*," with authority, with not even the slightest insinuation of a question mark at the end of the word. By the end of the hour, I realized that I had to start training myself to issue commands more like an army sergeant than a plaintive friend. Mellow-voiced to the point where more than one person has suggested I go into phone sex if the whole journalism thing doesn't work out, I needed to make my FM radio voice heard through a haze of puppy distraction. I needed to project; the soggy bass needed to play lead. I felt like a fool talking so bossily to my dog, especially outside, when someone might hear me issuing orders, but I believed it was essential.

Simultaneously, I was studying all the training books—by Cesar Millan, by the Monks of New Skete—about taking charge of your dog, who was once a wolf. They made me feel even more that I had to be commanding, or else Toby could ruin our finely tuned balance, our vertical control, our brightness, our sharpness. We were two men with demanding jobs—I worked mostly at home; Tom went to the office—already straining to maintain our well-earned stability. With the advent of Toby, I was scrambling to keep up with my TV shows, to have sustained thinking and writing time, to have something to say to my zeitgeist-addicted editors and to my readers about the nondoggy universe. In those first weeks and months of Tobyworld, my sense of control was under siege.

———

That I was in such close proximity to a dog, even enjoying his breath on my face, was a little absurd. Here's the way back-story: For most of my life, I hated dogs, all dogs. I was terrified of them, so much so that I once slept in the bathroom rather than face my roommate's visiting dog, who waited for me outside the bathroom door, panting, barking, whining, hoping to play with a new friend. I was in college and living off campus, and my roommate was out, so I dozed sitting up, my neck against a roll of toilet paper, until she came home at four in the morning, whereupon I pretended that I just happened to be using the toilet at that moment. "Oh, hey, good morning, good night," I said with blurry eyes to her and her dog, a German shepherd mix, who was now wagging his tail at her, as I walked out of the bathroom. I was afraid of things that moved quickly and unpredictably—not just dogs, but basketballs and base-balls, speedboats, love, anything that could abruptly invade my personal space and crack the glass.

As a teen, I spent most of my time stoned, and stonelike, a statue with wide, vacant eyes, mouth shut. My face was pale, angular, wary of the playful spirit. Forever bored, I'd sit rubbing joint and cigarette ashes into my jeans and listening to cerebral rock 'n' roll with friends. I'd get drunk and laugh my stomach sore, and then, the next day, return to my mope. My mother foisted me on my older brother David for a week during his freshman year at Lehigh University, and he was unnerved by my clenched blankness around his new friends, all of them newly and giddily out of the nest. "At least keep your mouth open when you sit there," he begged.

I was morbidly afraid of playing sports, and forged gym notes at school on a regular basis, adding the feminine curlicues that I thought befitting a pretty young mother. Soccer, football, Ping-Pong—the ball would race back and forth and over and up, and I'd feel unprotected, stupid, trapped in a secret hell of dread. Amid the rampant motion of a basketball game in which I was forced to play at school or summer camp, I'd go into emotional lockdown. I must have looked like a human bomb shelter to the sports teachers, all clenched against flying things. One glance at the basketball court and you'd spot me and think, Major geek and freak. Play frightened me, and it mystified my early sense of reason—I just couldn't see the reward in letting go, in running around a field in sneakers and risking damage and embarrassment. I may have seemed like the proverbial "old soul," but I was more of a scared child.

And dogs were like dodgeballs with teeth and bad breath. The idea of playing around with a dog was unthinkable. I was afraid of all dogs, from bossy Malteses to gentle Great Danes. When I was seven or eight, I had a recurring nightmare about being chased by a Saint Bernard while riding my bike on Plymouth Street, a few blocks from our home in New Bedford, Massachusetts. The dog's head was giant and tufted and he was nipping at my heels as I pedaled desperately onward. I could see throbbing red veins in his eyes. He chased me uphill, hundreds of pounds of teeth, jowls, and foamy spittle. This wasn't a W. C. Fields mascot with a small barrel of brandy around his neck; this was Cujo, and he was running me out of suburbia. His expression didn't convey the bored loyalty of the classic Saint Bernard; it reflected fury at me and my bike-riding ass. He wasn't forcing me to go home; he was banishing me. The dog—and, by extension, all dogs—kept me from where I belonged. He was driving me off to the land of parentlessness, shame, and death. Yeah, it cut deep.

Around the same time, I saw the local animal officers lead a rabid mutt out of my neighbor's front bushes with a contraption that looked like a fishing rod with a carrot on the end. It was after school, and I watched safely from the brick front steps in my yard two houses away. I expected to see a ferocious beast emerge from the arborvitae, shooting sparks and clawing at the air, but the dog was listless and spent. His hind legs looked rubbery, and he seemed to be pulling himself forward with his front legs, slouching toward his doom. *Rabid.* The word forever fixed itself in my brain beside *dog.* Dogs are lame and dirty; dogs want to chase you down; dogs have a crazy disease that can infect you. If I ever accidentally touched a dog at a friend's house, or touched something that had touched a dog, my hand would quietly buzz until I could wash it and turn off the alarm. An older kid in fifth grade had once told me that if you visualized a dog attacking you in the presence of a dog, you would, in fact, get attacked, so my negative thoughts became more inescapable because they were so powerful.

"Go-wan!" was what my frightened mother would half-yell at any neighborhood dog that came close to her on the street, as in "Shoo, go on." Usually composed, gentle, and fashionable, she'd try to wave them away as she would a fly, stepping back awkwardly in case her warnings were impotent, looking very alone. She and I both backed away from play and haphazard movement; when your guard is down, we knew, precious things are stolen—my father, for example, whose unremarkable flu had quickly devolved into early death from a rare blood disease. Both of us were steeled against more sudden plunder.

Fear—it's the birth of winter, the frozen root, the hands lifted so they won't get bitten, as if frost doesn't reach above a certain height.

But I found Tom in 1998, and he pried me out of my retreat. I'd always expected that I couldn't love, that I was afraid to love because I was afraid to lose, that I was a hybrid of clichés about literary types who can't let go, grievers who can't move on, and TV addicts whose souls are as slippery as the aisles of a chain store. I'd always expected I would wave my hand and say "Gowan," like my mother, to any eager suitor twitching his nose at me and signaling me to come frolic.

I was wrong.

And with Tom, and his gushy, melancholy Irish temperament, always ready for a sentimental moment, I found dogs. There's a comedy album from the 1960s called *When You're in Love the Whole World Is Jewish.* For me, falling in love made me and the whole world into dog lovers. When I fell in love with Tom, when he made his way through my cool desolation, something in me in fell apart; a wall or two crumbled. Some people learn to love a dog and then a person; I came at that backward. Once in the world of contact, in love with a human being, I felt more at ease around the uncontrollability of an animal. Tom's doting aunt, who lived an hour away in Bedford, had a border collie and three poodles; her old three-story house was ruled by this fab four, and a few cats. And Tom still grieved his golden retriever, Teddy, tearing up at the mention of his name. His brother had a wise yellow Lab elder. A friend had gotten a Samoyed, a feisty fluff ball. After a lifetime dodging dogs, I began to feel more secure and open around them. The longer I stayed in love with Tom, the more I could rock and roll and improvise. Embracing a dog, like embracing a person, is taking on the unpredictable, the mysterious, the joyous, and, someday, the terrible.

For a few years, Tom pressed me for a dog, but I was anxious about what would happen to our lovely sense of order, the ménage a trois between Tom, me, and the TV. There was only a certain amount of love to go around, it seemed, once all of my TV work was done. That's why I kept saying no; I felt love and devotion toward him, but what if those feelings came in limited amounts? But my resistance eroded. I'd been wrong before, and, after dog-sitting a friend's spectacular black-and-white lady mutt named Bailey for a weekend, I began to find the thought of never owning a dog unbearable. It felt like I'd had a best friend over for a weekend. When Bailey's owner came to pick her up on Sunday, she ran to him, and I was a little crushed. The minute they left and the door closed, I put a big frown on my face.

"I miss Bailey," I said, and Tom laughed at me, enjoying his triumph.

That holiday season, I gave Tom one of those cards with a close-up of a puppy on the front—dog-owner pornography, card-manufacturer shamelessness—and inside I wrote simply "OK," as in "I'll be okay," "We'll be okay," and "Okay, let's get a dog."

sidewalk traffic

Like every puppy, Toby required lots of outdoor walking in the process of toilet training—even in the middle of the night, for which I let go of my addiction to earplugs, those heavenly little foam capsules that force the world to recede into calm and quiet. Now I needed to listen for soft, dissonant whimpers from the crate by our bed, then carry him down to the street (or pretend I was still sleeping and wait to hear Tom take him down). The first night Toby was at our apartment, I slept on the floor in front of the crate so he could see my face, sure that he was still distressed by the ride from New Hampshire. By night two, after a day watching Toby achieve new heights of joy and cuteness with a variety of toys, I let go of my childhood-trauma abandonment projection and got back in the bed.

In the middle of the night, I sometimes enjoyed leading Toby on a leash around the blocks of our Brookline neighborhood, a mixture of old wood-sided houses and three- and four-story brick apartment buildings. It was ghostly, two creatures ambling through the quiet, the charcoal sky glazed with orange, Toby batting and then scampering after chunks of mulch and cigarette butts as if it were a sunny morning. There's a little universe of detritus along city sidewalks, if you see them through a dog's eyes—bottle caps, chicken bones, dead lighters, ads from the weeklies, a blackened penny every now and then.

Daylight walking was a different kind of scene, based around a more complicated traffic grid of near misses, apologetic nods, and head-on encounters, as Toby would stop suddenly to sniff a bush or a tree trunk or jump up like a yo-yo at a pedestrian. Who knew the sidewalk could be such a fraught place? I sometimes felt as though I was leading a vacuum cleaner bumpity-bump down the sidewalk, and watching the on-comers choose their approach. Some, the sidewalk warriors, would absolutely refuse to veer from their path when they spotted Toby and me ahead, continuing straight into us, maybe even picking up speed. I once was such a warrior, looking dully at the dog in my path and forging onward, businesslike, slightly hostile.

The sidewalk worriers were a problem, too. They'd veer when they saw Toby and me. They'd veer in a big way. They'd go into the street and around the outside of cars, if needed, in order to avoid the man and the frightening dog. The man: six one, 165 pounds, brown hair, a big snout. The dog: then about thirty-five pounds, fair, also with a plus-size snout. Both were harmless. But the worriers—I'd been one of them, too—didn't know the difference between a tetchy dachshund, an elderly mutt, and a lighthearted yellow Lab. They simply made their way around us, half-smiling nervously as they headed off course. "Sorry," they'd mumble.

They'd work their internal rudders ably, looping casually as if, well, that was just part of city walking. Toby's tail would start swinging at the sight of them—PEOPLE!—but they were immune to his charms. They didn't deliver attitude, and they'd have apology playing around their clamped-down mouths as they fled us. They owned their ignorance of dogs affably—the "silly me" position. But they made me feel guilty, a bit like a monster pedestrian.

One day, a sidewalk worrier approached with her four- or five-year-old child. Both were clearly afraid of dogs—fear from the mother siphoned to the son; I knew the signs—but they still moved toward us slowly, as if walking the plank, holding their hands up, making Toby think they had something special for him in their palms. "Hi, I'm so sorry," the mother said with a stricken face. Innocence clashed as Toby pulled at the leash, jumping ecstatically, and the adorable kid with a cartoon T-shirt tiptoed toward him in tears. It was just too much. I felt cornered on the sidewalk. I apologized, pulling at Toby's leash, then had a flash of annoyance—irrationally so, since I, more than most dog owners, had a profound understanding of the fear of dogs.

So it was a fantastic coincidence when, on a walk later that day, I met Leslie. She drove up beside Toby and me across from our apartment, opened her window, and asked, "Can I say hello to that adorable puppy?" She pulled over, jumped out, and took in Toby like she'd just gotten to the water's surface after a deep dive and was inhaling at last. He jumped at her knees while she knelt in jeans, both petting his head with her knuckly fingers and pulling her many-braceleted, jangly arms away from his love bites. Leslie, who looked like a wheaten terrier with her dirty blond bangs and calm, freckly face, urged me to socialize Toby with other dogs. "You should take him to Amory Park," she said. "It's a whole scene."

"I'm focusing on training him," I said with newbie pride and a touch of smugness born of all my dog-guide reading. "They say Labs need to be taught early."

"They also need to play!" She said it with a squeal to Toby, stretching out the word *play* as if she were saying "Weeeee!" to a toddler, and his tail double-timed. She repeated the word, again sounding like a party horn—"plaaaayyy"—and Toby's tail again swung faster. They both knew it was obvious: play-time with others.

They were right. Leslie had pointed out the flaw in my plan— Tom and I as a semi-closed-off system, the fabulous gay couple with the dog as polite child, a family unit with well-paged copies of *Puppies for Dummies*. I knew I needed to find an urban subculture of dog people, away from the complexities of the sidewalk warriors and the sidewalk worriers. I needed to give that to Toby as his urge to play with other dogs and observe and imitate their behavior continued to grow. But of course I wasn't much of a joiner, even as I'd wandered in and out of various fringe groups over the years. I remember going to the 1992 Rainbow Gathering, an annual peace and love hippie event, looking for connection and a sense of fellowship. Amid unasked-for hugs, the constant greeting of "Welcome home, brother" from strangers, and born-again-Christian leaflets mysteriously and creepily appearing in my camping gear, I felt burdened by my TV-bred irony and my independence. One afternoon on a grassy knoll, I overheard a bearded wisp of a man working to hawk up every millimeter of phlegm in his lungs, trying to cleanse himself, sounding like a lawn mower that wouldn't start. I could go with the cult flow only so far before I felt hipstery and urban, before I wanted to trash-talk the Krishnas, eat a Twinkie, and pull out the most forbidden of items: money.

But while standing on the sidewalk talking to Leslie, my urban space suit—the cynical barrier between me and strangers—was feeling like a puffed-up down jacket in summer. She was Glinda, the good witch, telling me to get my precious ass over to the land of Oz. And I knew in my heart that I needed to give Toby the familial embrace of group formation, a chance to find his place among his own "people." So, grudgingly, baggage in tow, I scheduled a break from my digital leash and planned a trip to Amory.

the purell incident

When I mentioned that I would be going to Amory dog park to another dog owner I'd met a few times while walking Toby on my block, he rolled his eyes, smirked, and shook his head. "That's a weird place," he said, his standard poodle jumping back on all fours whenever little Toby sniffed at him. "Dog people can be pretty weird."

I was too ready to confirm his opinion when I made my first solo visit to Amory in early November. I didn't expect to fit in. It was my first big dog outing without Tom, and I perceived it as a training session, an opportunity to school Toby with some of the tips that Don, the trainer, had shown us. We'd work on "come," "stay," and the holy grail of commands, "drop." And the visit was a quiet disaster. I was thoroughly embracing the one-on-one with a dog, but the one-to-many was a bridge too far.

Tom, it needs to be said, was less obsessed with training. He stayed at the apartment that Saturday, having decided not to think about calmly asserting alpha status, intermittent treats, or the correct way to issue a command (saying "Toby" before the command). He was getting tired of the word *command,* tired of my commitment to raising the perfectly controlled dog, ready to say "tssst" to Cesar Millan. He'd had dogs all his life, and none of them had needed to be rigorously trained, but I was gung ho about making sure Toby would be a well-behaved canine and not pure wild nature. Maybe I was more than gung ho, as I highlighted passages in training manuals and signed us up for a beginner's training class at the Brookline VFW hall for the following month. I was afraid back then that if our dog was a beggar or a jumper, friends without dogs would no longer want to visit us, that somehow having an excitable dog would be perceived as a personal failing; Tom was very "love me, love my dog." For me, treats were rewards; for Tom, treats were a way of life, whereby Toby would get a cookie for leaving the apartment, returning to the apartment, getting in the car, hopping onto the couch, going into one of his many crates, and many other mundane "accomplishments."

"Remember what Don said about how too many treats makes them less powerful," I'd say to Tom, and he'd look at Toby and say, "We don't care about Don, do we Toby, do we?" And then, with dog ventriloquism, Tom would have Toby answer, "No, we don't care about Don." I didn't want our daily existence with a dog to become an endless series of collisions and confrontations, like a football game. I was in love with Toby but was feeling more like a junior-pageant stage mother from the abominable reality show *Toddlers & Tiaras* than I was willing to admit.

Tom and I had taken Toby to Amory together very briefly the previous week, as a test visit, after Leslie had told me about it. We'd stuck to our own corner of the large squarish park, watching Toby bite on and play with a tennis ball, tentatively mingling with a woman named Margo and her setter mix, Travis. With her nest of red hair and black-rimmed rectangular glasses, Margo had ambled toward us and started talking politics and dog park rules. She was nice and energetic, and, like so many dog owners, she looked something like her dog, who sat avidly biting his tennis ball, ignoring Toby's attempts to nip him and mobilize him. Both were perky redheads.

But still we felt invaded, and early in the conversation we politely withdrew to the car.

"Well, I have no need to go back there," Tom said as we drove home. The park didn't suit him; he preferred to bond with Toby on meandering walks, a chord with two notes, or by taking him to the beach. Silently, I disagreed with him. Unlike me, Tom didn't have an ominous sense about the park, which, if fears are wedded to wishes, meant he didn't much desire to be there, either. With his beloved collection of sappy, yellowed books from the early 1900s about noble farm mutts—I think he even once suggested we name Toby Yeller—he was a "one man dog" type of guy. I felt a nascent curiosity about fitting in with a group, about finding my spot, which he didn't. "Then I'll take him alone," I said, turning to pet Toby in the backseat.

Pulling into an Amory parking space that first day without Tom, Toby attentive in the backseat, I saw the field laid open before us in classic late-fall beauty. Many of the gray trees bordering the field were bare, and the sky showing through them was a deep blue. Toby was beaming at the sight, looking out from the rear door window with fire in his eyes.

The sight: Amory looked a bit like a sprawling courtyard, bordered by a low castlelike apartment building, a few gracious old stucco mansions, and a fenced-in nature preserve of woods with a pond. In the middle of the density of Boston University dorms, pizza restaurants, sports stores, and Beacon Street and Commonwealth Avenue trolley tracks, there was this sweet respite. A row of weeping willows lined a side of the park, hanging lazily over stray picnic tables as if in a fairy tale. How could I never have noticed a roughly eight-acre chunk of green only blocks from my apartment? That's the power of the digital bubble, I thought, where you can watch faraway monster fish attack on the National Geographic Channel and still be unconnected to the nature in your backyard. Amory—its physical beauty—was one of the first unexpected things that Toby, through Leslie, had brought me. And it was distinctly Boston. I noticed that, behind the grassy Amory field, you could see the Prudential Tower—Boston's favorite ugly icon, an old hibachi grill on its side and crowned with a fifties Martian cap. It reached high in the far backdrop.

In the middle of Amory, the baseball diamonds faced away from each other, their outfields overlapping and spreading out into a no-man's-land for Frisbee, football throwing, and, that day, the constellation of people and dogs running among them like shooting stars.

Summoning my new authoritative voice—"Don't ask, tell," trainer Don had told us with a smirk—I opened the back door and made Toby sit, blocking his exit from the car, his chubby blond body trembling to run. I attached his leash and released him from the backseat, saying, "Okay, go!" We walked from the lot onto the field and I tried to make him sit again, to settle him down, before unclipping the leash. Nope, he wasn't having it, not at this close distance to other dogs, and no matter how severe I became, no matter how many times I repeated "Sit," he ignored me.

We stood there, at odds, Toby pulling frantically, unaware of my frustration. I had to win this one. I finally just pushed his tush down, said a token "Sit," and detached the leash with my free hand, and in an instant he was puppy-galloping directly toward the dozen or so dogs in the baseball outfield, his velvety ears flip-flopping in syncopation over his head. I wasn't even a memory to him.

I watched him with a rare uncontainable smile on my face, miffed at the way he'd ignored my command but nonetheless touched by his exhilaration. If he'd been a kid, he would have been skipping. He was on his way to fun school. Margo, peering through her rectangular glasses, saw him coming across the grass, pointed him out, and she and the other dog owners all cheered and giggled like a sitcom audience. Dogs make the heart sing; puppies make the voice sing, too.

And then, on his big journey toward the clutch of life at the center of the field, Toby stopped and squatted in one swift motion, his enthusiasm barely abating as a few miniature logs slid out. Only a puppy can poop before a crowd with the casual reflex of a guy tucking a strand of hair behind his ear. The owners laughed louder, and Toby resumed his skipping, an ounce or two lighter. There was not a fiber of fear or embarrassment in him as he faced the specter of human and dog attention. Tom and I had taken him home from Mirabelle Labs at an age—seven weeks—when he was ready to bond with us, and trust us, as if the possibility of not trusting us didn't exist. We stared warmly into his brown-sugar eyes every day as we carried him up and down the two flights of stairs at our apart-

ment building, quietly saying his name to his face, and he looked
back into our eyes, unthreatened. "Toby, Toby," we'd say while
he stared back passively, step by step, "Toby."

It was the kind of innocent ignorance you want to preserve
for the duration of a dog's life. For my first dog—in what was a
misguided newbie effort to be in control, I realize, having since
loved so many rescue dogs—I wanted to get a purebred dog for
the opportunity to witness this kind of tabula rasa. As he ran
off to play after having publicly pooped, I saw as unspoiled a
domesticated creature as I'd ever seen.

One of the high dog park decrees, written on all park signs and
at all doggie Web sites, fixated upon by owners and nonown-
ers, is that you must pick up after your dog.

As Margo explained to Tom and me during our quick first
visit to Amory, picking up gives less ammunition to the antidog
factions, which don't like dogs running free in the parks. And,
obviously, it protects park users from painstakingly having to
scrape shit out of the ridges on the bottoms of their shoes. So I
made a big display of doing my job that Saturday morning, letting the others know I knew. Lagging behind Toby, I pulled a
crinkled Star Market bag out of my pocket, bent over slightly,
looked down carefully, and plucked up the poop, the bag like
a raincoat over my hand.

What I was performing was poop mime, which responsible
dog owners seem to do when others might be watching. "See,"
says your thought balloon as you conspicuously hold your bag
out for all to see, "I'm a good citizen." You are a flagrant goody-
goody for a moment, an upholder of the social contract. You

step forward like a silent-film actor, bag fluctuating in the breeze, quite visibly game to retrieve whatever your little darling has delivered. Oh, there it is! Hooray! And bend over, and grab, and scene.

Picking up, I could feel the slight, deadweight of Toby's warm turds, a thin layer of plastic protecting my fingers. Or was it protecting my fingers?

Since I'd started walking Toby around the neighborhood, teaching him to poop outside instead of the next-closest thing—just inside our apartment door—I'd begun having lively conversations with myself about permeability. Are supermarket plastic bags porous on some level? Do they contain minuscule holes invisible to the human eye, like the finest, most infinitesimal of spaghetti strainers? The thought would poke at me beneath my proud new status as a first-time dog daddy. Are evil molecule-size beings taking up residence in my fingerprints, embedding themselves between each groove? I was getting more and more dependent on hand sanitizer every week, carrying a small plastic bottle with me along with my keys and wallet. Thanks to Purell, my hands were clean but dried-out and coarse, with hieroglyphic breaks on my knuckles. Ah, the cold sting of a few clear, gelatinous drops!

Once, I made Tom sanitize his hands before hugging me, since he'd walked the dog earlier that night. He laughed his "Next time, I won't laugh" laugh.

I dropped the knotted bag in a barrel and jogged over to where Toby was being sniffed by his elders, who included Bertha, a golden retriever owned by a scruffy-faced guy named Nash, and Travis, Margo's setter mix. I knew I, too, was about to be sniffed, in a manner of speaking, as Margo approached with a wide, inquiring smile that revealed a little lipstick on her teeth, asking the standard questions: "What's his name again?" "How old is he?" And, since he is a yellow Lab, "Have you read *Marley & Me*?" On the sidewalk, kids and parents were already pointing at my "Marley," and I had to stop myself from responding, "No, he's a Toby" in defense of my puppy's still-forming identity. In fact, there is a story called "Toby Dog," by Rudyard Kipling, but, alas, it never became a Jennifer Aniston movie and it didn't initiate a market tidal wave of dog books. It sits in Tom's shelf of old books, musty and brittle, a resale price of fifty cents penciled in on the opening page.

Margo reminded me that her dog was Travis, who was now intently mouthing a tennis ball near my feet. With his droopy rust red ears and long rust red coat, Travis looked like a Hacky Sack–playing hippie jam bander. He had a narrow, athletic build, and his limbs were limber. As I answered Margo's questions, Travis caught a whiff of the dog cookies in my pocket, dropped his ball, and jumped up on my leg, his paws leaving long streaks of cold mud on my clean pants.

"I'm sorry," Margo said to me, half meaning it, pulling Travis away by his collar, and I said, "It's okay," half meaning it, stepping back. The whole getting mucked-up thing, which is inevitable in the muddy fall and spring, was new to me. You had to dress for mess at the dog park, I soon learned; if you didn't and your fancy pants got marked up by dog drool and a cold, wet nose pressed against your cookie pocket, it was your own fault.

Other owners came over to hear about the new puppy, and Toby jumped at them and darted through their legs. To him, they were a Stonehenge to run in and out of.

"Where's your partner?" Margo asked, and I explained that Tom, my husband—"Congratulations!" she exclaimed—was busy at home. I stood by awkwardly, my smile becoming a bit forced. Did any of them notice I was holding my right hand by my side, feeling my corduroy jacket pockets with my left hand for a magic bottle of sanitizer? No. They had smiling faces, and soon I would get to know a few of them well: Margo; Bertha's owner, Nash, always poised, Groucho Marx–like, to make a joke; Ky, the stoned poet with the boxer mix and the brown eyes; Hayley, with her long, thick brunette mane and her Bernese mountain dog, Stewie; and a hyperactive woman named Noreen, talking and talking, always talking, about TV. But at the time, they were a blurred group of strangers looking for small talk and distracting me from my goal: to disinfect.

After Toby had exposed his soft, vulnerable belly to all interested parties, he started bouncing from dog to dog. He had clearly found his homeland, the place where he saw others of his kind and fit in. I watched a sense of belonging fill him up that day and charge his entire body with life. He was becoming more of who he would be—the master of tennis balls and squeaky toys, a playful, eternal boy. His paws, still so out of proportion to the rest of his body, were caked with park mud as he jumped at whatever was near him, dog or human, and he was in ecstasy. He looked like he was wearing black socks.

Every so often, he'd return to me and look at me in the eye as if to say, "Can you BELIEVE this?" And yet there I was in a circle of hell, triggered by what I'd seen on some overblown Discovery Channel series about bacteria making a fantastic voyage up to the brain and wrecking the entire order of a life—vision clouded by a flowering parasite, thinking turned rabid.

I'd begun using both hands to reach deep into the compartments of my corduroy jacket, pulling out an extra poop bag, a phone, a few tissues. But I could not come up with my precious plastic bottle; when leaving the apartment, I'd put on a warmer jacket and forgotten to pack it properly. Toby had thrown even the tiniest details of my life off. Generally, I organized my pockets as if they were safety-deposit boxes of small treasures.

And thus my quiet disaster. I could see the group begin to watch my hands in motion as they continued talking to me, as if all was normal. Margo said she was glad I'd decided to socialize Toby properly by coming to the park. And I nodded in agreement, my eye contact sporadic. "Yes, puppy fur smells so fresh." "Yes, they sleep a lot." "No, you can never take too many pictures." "I got him in New Hampshire."

Toby had settled into one-on-one play with Bertha, whose golden retriever head was an oversized, furrier version of his. He was shades brighter than she, his coat still velvety and fuzzy. He sprung up at her ear and her densely furry throat, biting and biting. Many golden retrievers are bred to have coats on the blonder side of red, but Bertha was on the redder side of blond. She stood still, moving her head and neck from side to side in a halfhearted effort to dodge Toby's rigorous snaps. She squealed, too—it seemed she was squealing with pain, since Toby's teeth were minuscule ice picks and his control over his bite was still inexact. Is he puncturing Bertha's flesh and drawing blood? I wondered. Another permeability issue, along with my terror of germs in my bloodstream. But as

I mumbled apologies in the midst of my search for Purell, Nash explained that Bertha was playing the tolerant teacher.

"She'd put a stop to it, if she wanted to," he said. "She's not shy. She's just mentoring the newbie." He nodded knowingly at me, trying to look past my turmoil. Still, I could see mystification playing vaguely around his eyes. He wanted to move on, to find the next joke with the group. But I was stuck.

"Does anyone happen to have any hand sanitizer?" I finally blurted it out, trying, unsuccessfully, to put a chuckle in my voice. I looked at the park people, and they looked at me. We were all still, as a beat passed, only the dogs in motion, unfazed. My neurosis had leaked through my reserve. I was weird, and everyone could see it. When writing for the *Globe,* I was usually able to keep my hang-ups out of my copy, or deploy them comically; but in person, I had a lot less self-command.

Maternal above all, Margo actually put her hands in her pockets, saying, "I don't think so." Seeing her, a few of the dogs, including Bertha, stopped what they were doing and came trotting over, certain she was going to pull out treats for them. Nash looked down at Bertha, avoiding eye contact with me. He and a few others very slowly fell back into conversation, where the subject was probably something like puffed-up Officer Marv, or the recent Red Sox championship season. Only a guy named Ky was crazy enough to take me on, fixing his bloodshot brown eyes on my face and saying, "Hey, what's the sanitizer for?" He had a thick ponytail, which was in an informal braid with lots of stray frizz around it.

"I just hate the thought of getting shit on my hands."

"These guys are poop machines," Ky said. "The food goes

in; the shit comes out. It's part of nature. Don't worry about it." He smiled at me.

"I hear you," I said, but my tone was kind of a blow-off. "I think my bag may have had a hole in it." I felt like a fool. I looked like an uptight newcomer, and maybe I was. I saw myself and squirmed. Ky smiled at me and said, "Yeah, the bags are useless." He added, "Stay cool now," and walked away.

I grabbed the leash, which had been coiled in my pocket, and moved toward Toby, who was still going at Bertha, blissfully unaware of my predicament. I was ready to round him up and walk on, maybe circle the field once or twice, practice training exercises, and get back to the car. I was ready to decontaminate, and catch up on my TV viewing while Tom took over the Toby watch for an hour or two. I can't allow this place into my life, I thought—which was the same way I'd once felt about dogs in general.

I felt completely impermeable that day, unable to let my guard down and allow this new scenario in. But somewhere in the back of my mind as I attached Toby to the leash and led him away from the pack while he tugged against me to continue playing, I nonetheless knew I was heading into something messy. At some point, I understood that, despite my exodus, I would have to let Toby run free and allow my hands to get dirty.

pack of freaks

When I got home that day, I washed my hands, partially aware of how ludicrous I had been. I realized that I'd had one of those experiences where you are driven into a narcissistic state by social discomfort. Instead of accepting the overtures of Margo, Nash, Ky, and the others, I'd spent the hour worrying about invisible germs on my hands.

"You'll be wearing gloves soon enough," Tom said when I told him, and we laughed at the absurdity of it. But he even went to the closet for me and pulled out our collection of orphaned and matching winter gloves.

Toby and I returned to the park on Monday, and I thought I should make an effort to be a little more available to new faces. But once again, I blew the experience, as the dog park people I encountered that day seemed particularly hectic and lacking in boundaries. I fell into a defensive position, what I now know is a common response to a dog park. If you watched the park entrance during puppy season—usually from May to October—you saw people like me making their first visits, wary and weirded-out, uncomfortable when strangers started to make conversation with them.

Once again, I tried to get Toby to sit when we walked onto the field, before unleashing him, per Don's instructions. Once again, he ignored me, the little bugger, so completely convinced that I was not paying attention to the glories that lay mere feet away. Whichever brain department responds to pleasure stimuli such as giant bacon strips and rubber squeaky toys and wrestling in the grass, that department in Toby was fully mobilized. In his panting, crying, uncontainable excitement, I didn't exist for him. He was thoroughly in the moment of yearning. Again I announced "Sit"; again I sounded whiny; again I was powerless. I pushed his tush down, said "Sit," and unhooked him in defeat. He tore ahead, his lanky legs in full throttle, heading toward a guy and his dog alone under the weeping willows.

The guy stood by the picnic tables in jeans, cowboy hat, and dried-out pale orange Tyroleans. As I approached in the wake of Toby, I detected a hint of patchouli in the air around him, mixed with eau de fall mud and the smoke from his Camel Light. He had puffy green eyes and old acne scars, and, as he took a drag of his cigarette, I could see that his long hands were strafed with scratches and calluses. His stiff old girl sat by his feet, looking up at me, her tail thumping against the dirt. Toby had slowed his run and walked up to her tentatively, stretched out his neck, and began sniffing at her giant light brown head, his black nostrils flexing and his tail swinging with his inhalations. He was still a wide-eyed student of the canine class system, but he nonetheless understood that she was not to be jumped upon as if she were another puppy. And she had eyes only for me, waiting for a pat and a cookie. I obliged.

"Thanks," the guy said, and I nodded and smiled as I knelt and scratched behind her ear. "That's Maya. She's getting up there, and less apt to stand up. She's about fourteen, but we got her as a rescue, so I really don't have any exact info. We think she's part Lab, part ridgeback, but who knows. She's been a great dog, that's for sure. She's been as loyal"—did his eyes fill slightly?—"as, you know, a best friend. And that's why we love them, right?" He puffed his Camel. I nodded, standing up again and looking down at Toby. "Best friends. If I walked through that patch of mud over there, she'd follow me, right at my heels, no questions asked, you know? Maya is my best girl." She looked up at him and her tail hit against the ground again, slap-slap-slap. Toby, meanwhile, came and sat politely at my feet, maybe tired from the excitement of getting to the park, maybe just mirroring Maya's ease.

"I got her in the divorce, and we've gotten really close," the guy continued. "Really close. She wanted to come with me; I'm sure of it, although my ex didn't think so. Every time Maya stayed at my ex's new apartment, she peed all over everything!" Another puff, more wags as I laughed. "I think that was her statement of intent. She just peed her way out of my ex's life. Now she's all mine. The thing about my ex is that she's not a dog person. Not really. She's a fair-weather friend to dogs, put it that way. So Maya comes to work with me every day. I'm in construction, so she just waits in my truck, happy as can be. We're working on a site right near here, so it's perfect. Of course she used to run around, but now not so much. Now my Maya hangs tight." Wag, wag, wag.

"My ex won't get to say good-bye, that's all. She's done with us. I tried to tell her that there isn't much time left, but she's tired of listening to me. She pushed me out the door, done with me." I pressed my lips together and then started to mutter sympathies, but he continued. "We tried counseling, but she felt I was an angry person. So we both moved out, and I'm in a studio apartment with Maya for the time being." Wag, wag, wag. "She's my best girl."

Well, um, nice to meet you, I thought. He looked at his phone, and, before I could form a full sentence, the guy—I never learned his name—was saying good-bye, helping Maya up, and leading her back along the path from the picnic tables to his truck. I began to ponder his need to divulge as Toby and I continued on the outer loop of the Amory field, Toby jumping at my side to bite at my hand as we headed toward some activity farther on. Talk about boundary issues, I thought. I'd merely said hello, and he'd proceeded to dump a full load of personal information on me. Talking to a man with a still face and a friendly puppy, the guy had had an inappropriate confessional catharsis.

Dam burstage: It was one of the great lures of the park, I learned early on, the liberation of anonymity, the freedom of having no name. Dams can burst unexpectedly and overwhelmingly when you're off the record, among strangers and a collection of animals who'll love you no matter what. Sometimes, it was a sweet venting event, narrating your life to a person you might never see again, not worrying about consequences and not caring about judgment. I'm certain that the nearness of dogs, with their naked vocal and facial expressions, so unconcerned with covering up, opens the heart for some people. That day, though, as I stood listening while my first park dam burstage washed over me, I felt bombarded.

We ran into Margo and her explosion of red hair. She was the picture of dog-park shagginess. Under her jean jacket, she wore an oversized purple T-shirt with a thick leather belt outside of it, like a tool belt around her waist. The belt held up a dirty nylon treat sack, a few empty plastic supermarket bags, and a gnawed rope toy, and she held a red Chuckit ball thrower in her hand. People at the dog park carried these candy-colored Chuckits as if they were armed with cartoon weapons, lashing them forward as if to say, Take that, air. Travis walked behind her, staring intently at the ball sitting in the end of the Chuckit thrower that rested over Margo's shoulder, ignoring Toby as he jumped at his new friend. Below, Margo wore blue-plaid pajama bottoms, white socks, and brown leather clogs. There was a streak of dried toothpaste on her bottom lip.

She began to talk as she started flinging the dirty tennis ball for Travis, who sliced the air as he ran after it. Then Toby ran after Travis, the older dog's towheaded mini me, while Margo told me about the self-help book she was reading. "Meditation," she explained, "can cure all kinds of—" "Traaavis," she called out mid-sentence, "heeere" as Travis began going after another dog's red rubber ball, Toby still right behind him. "This book claims," she continued, as if she hadn't just yelled in my face, her eyes still on Travis, "that meditation can turn your health around and—" She stopped again. Now she brought out a silver whistle from her jacket's breast pocket and, saying a quick "Sorry," blew it hard. My ears shot up; Travis's didn't. Dropping the Chuckit, she then began waving her arms. "Travis here NOW," she screamed in a more staccato meter. She was a sweet lady with a spiritual bent, but then out of nowhere she was an army general barking orders. The buttons pinned like medals on the front of her jacket—PLANT A TREE; HUG A PERSON WHO HUGS A TREE—added to the militaristic effect.

As she went through her gyrations, a geometry problem gone wrong, still trying to carry on a narrative with me about her book while signaling her dog, I felt as if I were watching a late-night commercial for adult attention deficit disorder. *"If you can't focus, if you find simple tasks hard to finish, then you . . ."* Finally, she went after Travis and Toby, dropping her Chuckit on the ground by me, holding up a dog biscuit, and yelling out, "Cookie, Travis, cookie!"

Soon she was back, a Ping-Pong ball on the return. Travis had returned, too, to polite behavior, lying down and slobbering on his own tennis ball and not some stranger's fancy red toy. Toby jumped on Travis's back, throwing himself at his older playmate, but the ever-focused Travis continued to be disinterested—that, or he was enjoying his ball all the more, knowing he was being watched by an admirer. Another parallel with humans: The more others want something, the more value it seems to have. And Margo picked up where she'd left off, with meditation, modern life, the 24/7 pace, and the need to find respite. I agreed, and said, "It would be nice to spend at least a week without having Britney Spears in my face."

She squinched up her eyes at me. Was I talking about Prince Andrew's ex-wife? she wondered, because she really didn't pay much attention to all that royal drama.

"Oh, she's the new Madonna," I said, hoping to clarify the misunderstanding. "She's the latest pop icon."

"Ah, the classic figure, the holiest of females," she said, cocking her head a little, rectangular glasses atilt. "Jesus' mother, back in the public consciousness?" So what it came down to was that Margo didn't know who Madonna was. That was the strange truth. These figures, so primary in my world, continents on the map of global pop culture, were nowhere to her. Was she from another planet? She nodded along as I tried to explain Madonna, but I could tell she was faking her nods. She was ready to move on, to get back to the importance of healing.

Walking the Amory periphery, I began to feel like an early-twentieth-century psychiatrist touring a grassy sanatorium, in the midst of making a variety of diagnoses. Strange behavior seemed to spill out whenever I ran into someone at the park. I passed a small grouping, and Toby ran head-on into the middle of it. The owners all began laughing at his recklessness as he rolled and scampered, a blur of yellow. I walked over, and there was a woman named Noreen, talking to everyone at full volume, atonally, about *The Sopranos*. Bone-thin and wearing a silver-hooked nose ring, Noreen was like a wired fifteen-year-old. Her body language was speeded up, her memory acute.

"Remember when Tony and Carmela had their knock-down drag-out fight in the 'Whitecaps' episode?" she was saying to anyone who'd make eye contact with her. "That was a great moment of reckoning, right? That was the fifty-second episode of the series, and possibly the best." Meanwhile, her border collie mix crouched, waiting for her to throw her tennis ball, barking intermittently and swinging her eyes between Noreen and the ball in the longest, most obvious hint ever dropped. But Noreen was lost in her monologue. She was the epitome of a TV geek as she held forth, spewing a jubilant fountain of DVD-extra tidbits. In what seemed like a miracle of brain storage, she also had reams of useless data at the ready about 1970s sitcoms.

As I stood nearby, transfixed by Noreen's obsession with trivia and her extroversion in expressing it, watching Toby flit from dog to dog, looking for a play partner, an older woman with a fluffy bouffant introduced herself as Marcella.

"I can't stand listening to her," Marcella told me in a stage whisper, referring to Noreen. She said she wished her own dog, a cockapoo named Lady, would poop so she could leave. "Noreen gets under my skin, talking on and on about TV. Who cares what she has to say?"

She looked me in the eye and laughed, as if I automatically had agreed with her, which made me want to take Noreen's side. Marcella was one of those "I never watch TV" people, who, of course, as I'd learned over the years, do watch plenty of TV despite their shame. Once I told them what I did for a living, they had to scorn TV and let a beat pass before they started to tell me which shows they did like. In Marcella's case, she found time between teaching piano lessons at BU to watch the TV reality competitions that are set in exotic natural places.

The conversation ended with Marcella needling me for treating Toby like a child as I explained how Tom and I were in love with our little goose. I pointed to Toby and got a little mushy as I told her how much I already loved the little guy. "They're dogs," she said with an edgy giggle, "but not in this neighborhood!" She went on about the ridiculous plethora of dog books on the market, and the exorbitant amounts of money that people spend on dog toys, and I tuned her out and kept my eye on Toby. So negative, I thought, forgetting entirely that a few years earlier I might have said the same thing.

Fortunately, you can always extricate yourself from an unwanted situation at a dog park by suddenly becoming very, very interested in your dog—bungee jumping out with an excuse, such as "Oh, my dog is about to poop." I learned that practice very quickly. I bungeed out from Marcella, saying, "Toby and Lady are so cute together; look at them playing," and walked toward the pair as they wrestled fiercely, Lady's apricot fur shimmying and bouncing as she jumped and rolled, letting Toby get on top of her before swinging him over on his back. I leaped away from Marcella.

I felt sorry for Lady, and prayed she'd postpone her poop for as long as possible, since Marcella was impatiently waiting to leave. Why come to a dog park, I wondered, why even get a dog, if you don't want to bond with your pet, give him or her pleasure, maybe explore your own humanity? We create these breeds, set them off on their own without family like little orphans, and let them find a second family—us. And when they find us, often sent by plane and train to different parts of the country by rescue shelters, we need to let them in. I silently cheered Toby as he played with Lady, acting like my secret cohort and luring her into extremely non-poop-related activities as she chased him around all the people legs. Meanwhile, Marcella stood pouting in pearls.

That day, I also had my first encounter with Saul, a man of about eighty who ambled his way through the park with small but persistent steps.

Saul didn't have a dog, but he gravitated toward the dog people, who would take the time to talk to him as they stood on the grass or by the picnic tables. He wore a khaki beach hat, glasses with flip-up shades flipped up, and a weathered blue windbreaker as he moved among different groupings, always smiling and mumbling anecdotes.

Close-up, I could see that his shaving skills were getting spotty—there were little nicks and small patches of hair he'd missed—and that his jacket was stained with years of dirt and grease. His eyes would focus on you and yet not seem to register your specific image. "What kind of dog do you have there?" he asked me. I told him, he nodded, and then he started to tell me about his years working in some kind of crew capacity on a ship. Or maybe he was the captain. He got a sparkle in his eye as he talked, looking off like he was describing an especially vivid dream to me, viewing the broad, shining ocean from the bow of a rocking vessel. I suspected he was jumbling the facts. I asked questions, politely, but he wasn't attentive to them as he described eating boat food for extended periods of time.

"It wasn't fresh, but you got used to it," he said. "The guys and I liked to open those packages."

It's a peculiar position, when you've become the repository for a complete stranger's life stories, when you feel like a surrogate grandchild. I'm betting nurses go through it regularly. So I stood and listened, and listened, and listened, while Toby sat on the grass, resting, his chin on his paws, his eyes almost closing. I should have felt honored, and yet I could only feel sad. Saul seemed like a sweet but lost soul, adrift at the end of his life, that time when, in the common fantasy, we're all supposed to be held in the loving embrace of those who've known us.

Was I going to be like Saul one day? Had his face, now puffy and rounded, once been angular like mine? Those questions were playing in my subconscious. His deep nostalgia and what I perceived as a disconnected existence unsettled me. His hands were freckled with liver spots and his skin was sallow. I said good-bye and moved on, and he continued on his path around the park, looking for others to talk to, determined but rusting.

Later, by the parking lot, I ran into Margo, who was once again waving her arms and yelling out to attract the elusive Travis, who was now scrambling away from her, magnets of the same pole, whenever she approached. "I have to leave, but Travis won't come," she said as she moved in my direction. "I have a meeting!" She was heading to her car, her red hair blown back, hoping the threat of abandonment would persuade Travis. "Let's see if this does it," she said, pretending to be going to her car, yelling out, "Bye, Travis," and I wished her good luck with an invisible roll of my eyes.

Toby jumped into the backseat, and I made him sit before closing the car door. A good little soldier, I thought. I'll always have a handle on my guy, none of this epic battle of wills like Margo and Travis have, none of this rampant craziness. Between me, trainer Don, Cesar Millan, and the monks, I felt we'd have it covered. I was confused by the scene, by the way people intruded on my privacy, rushed my borders, let their dogs go out of control. I knew I had to come back for the dogs, but I wasn't in love with the idea of hanging out with the people. The freewheeling atmosphere of the park still felt too confused to me. And on another level, the day was like a warped reflection of my own fears—vanishing into TV like Noreen, the mystery of what getting old looks like answered by Saul. What bothers us about other people usually bothers us about ourselves, right?

I hadn't identified with Toby to the extent where if he was all about play and fun and jokes, then so was I. Our connection was still forming, strengthening each time he stole one of my socks and started running from the bedroom to the living room, each time he fell asleep on my foot like a little sack of weighted warmth. But his pleasure didn't give me the all-consuming pleasure it would in the coming weeks and months. The park seemed like a place where nuts gathered, where snobberies flourished, and where I would be the guy on the outside looking in.

And as I drove away, out of the parking lot and onto Amory Street, Toby panting behind me, I held my snout up just a little bit higher.

winter

dookie

But I kept going to the dog park, for Toby. Now that he'd had a taste of park joy, I couldn't deny him, even as the temperatures began to drop. Tom encouraged me to keep going, to help Toby get his energy out during the day; that way, we could all get mellow together at night.

When Tom got home from work, Toby would instantly pick up the nearest toy or sock and begin to run toward the dining room. Tom would say, "Oh, Toby boy!" put down his briefcase, and begin the chase that inevitably ended up going around and around the table—around and around, and then reverse, and then reverse again. Only after that exertion would Toby be willing to snuggle between Tom's legs as Tom lay back on the couch, a dog stretched out luxuriously on his back, limbs up, wrists bent, and slack belly exposed. We'd watch TV, but we'd really be watching Toby in disbelief, awed by his beauty.

My ignorance of dogs, I think, was charming to Tom. "You don't have to train a dog to get your shoe?" I asked one evening after he'd gotten home and finished the daily chase. It seemed

so odd to me that Toby would just do typically doggy things—
rest his head on a toy, bat around a ball with his paw, do a play
bow—without having gotten a lesson of some kind. I'd read so
many books about training, been so absorbed by the warnings
and the stories of how we can create aggressive dogs with poor
techniques, I believed that we truly shaped every facet of our
dogs, never mind about breed or temperament.

The more I pushed myself to take Toby to the park and mix,
the more, it seemed, I needed to work on Toby's training. It
was a control response, when faced with a daily bit of anarchy.
So every day, upon our arrival in the land of the unleashed,
standing at the entrance to the broad Amory field, I continued
to try to get him to sit for a moment before running off. There,
on the grass, I'd try to hold him back, to sober him up, to
delay his play for just a second, and he'd fight my effort with
every cell of forward energy in his irrational, hungry, impas-
sioned body.

It became our seminal owner-dog power struggle. We'd pull
off Amory Street at the park entrance and drive down the hill
into the parking lot, and I'd feel Toby wanting to run free.
He'd start pacing in the backseat of the car, crying deep in his
throat with pleasure at the sight of the hill and the weeping
willows and all that open space in the middle of the urban
density. And then we'd enact the same routine each time we
walked from the lot onto the field: I'd spit out, "Toby, sit."
Then I'd repeat the command in a military tone: "SIT." I'd hold
the leash tightly, a chewed-up green nylon thing, and he'd ignore my requests and heave onward to the grouping of people
and dogs on the grass, brown and yellow in patches as winter
approached. I'd try to keep him back, to exert control over

him before setting him loose, remembering Don's instructions. I wanted to teach him to have just one moment of centered calm before the hour of unbridled play. I wanted to be in command.

But he'd seen heaven just ahead and would look up at me like I was a fool for not rushing there. It was Tina Fey's catchphrase about innocent yearning from *30 Rock,* which she got from her young daughter: "I want to go to there." Toby's puppy determination was gorgeous as he'd run and run and bob his head forward despite the restraint from the leash in my hand and my repetitive verbal commands. He was in the early stages of being the comedian, a role toward people he later embraced the more he saw how his stubbornness made Tom and me laugh. Later on, he would become a willful clown with a sly smile, refusing to drop a ball and waiting for me to jokingly call him a "bad seed"; now, he was a happy little alien being discovering his own kind, beyond eager to ascertain the secret codes, most of them olfactory. He was in a state of headstrong glee, unaware of all humans, his body moving but not moving forward like a rocking horse, his paws scraping the grass. I could feel the pull of the leash in my hand in a regular pulselike rhythm, like jolts of gravity.

But I felt I had to hold him back, try to get him to focus on me. I had to win the contest, or else, I thought, Toby would never listen to me. Right? He would become a colossal pain, a rebel, chewing furniture and begging from and jumping on our houseguests, some of whom were not dog-friendly. I remembered how I'd hated to go to people's houses when they had a dog—the crazy movement, the spittle, the discomfort I felt while the dog was in the room, pretending I was okay with it. Toby would become a dogzilla. I'd read in one of the many guides I'd bought and studied that I should stare him down when he disobeyed, compel him into submission. So I'd try that when we'd arrive at the park, grasping his head and turning it toward mine, and I'd succeed at getting him to look away submissively, his eyes darting finally off to the side—but still, he would not willingly sit and wait for a few seconds before dashing off to freedom. I needed to assert authority over chaos, a need that, in retrospect, was maybe just a bit out of proportion to the moment. . . .

So is this to be our battleground, our stubborn point of difference? Is this to be our set piece, I wondered, like that same argument you have with your partner over and over and over again? My simple request, his simple refusal. My holding back, his growing desire. Tom and I had our own version of the set piece, and over the years we'd become experts at enacting it faster and faster, until it was just a flash, no longer a weekend of torment. For a few weeks, then, that was the point of contention with Toby, the "Sit" at the park. I couldn't just let go.

Standing in an urban paradise, a lovely hiatus from the surrounding glut of convenience stores and apartment buildings and traffic, enveloped by statuesque tree trunks and rocking limbs, the fragrance of dirt and fallen leaves in the air, a man tried and failed to face down an adorable yellow puppy.

How ridiculous we must have looked. I was working so hard to assert power, to be big and bad, pushing my soft voice to new levels of insistence; and he was oblivious to it. I was completely harmless in my wolf mask, and he knew it.

During the first two months at Amory, Toby and I kept crossing paths with Ky, who had thick brown eyebrows and long brown hair often pulled back in a braided ponytail. I liked him. He'd been there the day of the Purell incident, and I'd run into him and his boxer mix, Fritzie, a few times, but suddenly our park patterns were closely overlapping. He looked to be my first park friend. In his early thirties, he was stoned, usually, even in the morning, and he would ride his rusty red bike into the park from Cambridgeport, with Fritzie following him off-leash. He had high cheekbones, an irony-free smile, and he always wore the same too-small Mexican hoodie over a T-shirt, no matter how cold it was. I could smell his pot breath, earthy and sweet, although I'm sure most of the park people didn't notice it.

"Someone's been baking their breakfast," I'd say to him, and his face would brighten.

Unemployed and living with his social worker girlfriend, he freelanced, painting houses every now and then for cash. Fritzie was earthy, too. She would forage the park for a tennis ball, inevitably find one half-buried in mud, and trot around with it in a proud display. Meanwhile, Toby would trail her, while she ignored him, the eager tadpole. Actually, Fritzie pretended to ignore him; every so often, she'd throw a bark his way, or run close by him with the ball held high, to keep her loyal subject engaged.

Ky was a guy who had read Jack Kerouac and the Beat poets and spent time around a food co-op, and he had connected with a philosophy involving eating meat and no processed foods. He told me that he had once gone on a meat-only diet for a year, and it had solved all kinds of problems—skin rashes, colds, depression. "It was a chemical-free miracle," he said. He hated food packaging—"the waste industry." He was a believer in the purity of primitive life—that some things have been lost in our advancement and progress. And part of that approach involved honoring the cycle of birth and death, creation and dissolution, dust to dust, and, yes, food to shit. He fed Trixie a raw diet, no compromised kibble for her, and, I learned eventually, he felt that leaving her shit on the grass was part of the universal pattern. It goes in; it comes out—like the natural world breathing. His eyes were sincerely brown.

Ky was engaging, and he was adored by his girlfriend, who came to the park with him once and held his hand the whole time. She was clearly charmed by him and his passionate theories. And his perspective did have poetry to it, a limited ideal worldview that placed trust in the origins of mankind. I knew he was wrong not to pursue Trixie's poop, to just let her disappear into the trees on the hill and emerge a little lighter. Me, Mr. Antibacterial. But I thought he was a character, and I liked being in his confidence. Other people seemed uncomfortable around him, as he'd obsess over meat, attack fast-food chains, and grab hold of all the dogs—even strangers' dogs—while they played. Sometimes he'd draw disapproving looks when he'd pick up Trixie, who must have weighed fifty pounds, as though she were a giant, squirming infant. He'd pick up Toby, too, let Toby slime his face with his tongue, and laugh loudly. But I thought he was gentle and original, and I was starting to relax about going forward with an acquaintance at the park.

———

And then one day, it happened. Of course. We'd been talking about whether it was too late for the world, whether people would ever be willing or able to simplify in an age of instant gratification. He'd been condemning all of TV as a bad drug, an old argument I'd had a million times with a million different people, and we'd laughingly agreed to disagree.

Toby and I were walking away from him over a pile of wet brown leaves and I stepped smack in Fritzie's shit. I could tell by the golden color and soft, pâtélike consistency. I'd seen it before. It was her raw diet. The deathly smell made me gag as it mixed with the moldy, stinky leaves. I stood rubbing my boot against the ground, looking for a stick to scrape the sole. I was bent over, pushing Toby away from me to keep him clean, kicking and kicking my foot against the earth. And in my fluster, out of the corner of my eye, I saw Ky moving along, holding his bike while in conversation with someone else, smiling beatifically, fussing some more with the cosmic riddle. He looked like a caveman with a philosophy degree.

And it was then, watching him with great annoyance, no longer under his spell, that a park truism rose up from the dirt: "Those who pick up their dog's shit always step in shit. And those who don't, don't."

I actually thought of it as a "moral of the story" moment. Some of us think that karma will ultimately right the imbalances, that the self-righteous creeps and narcissistic takers and Zen poop strewers of the world will get their due before all is said and done. We fancy that someday Mr. Howell will lose his fortune, while Gilligan and his shovel win a Nobel Prize for keeping the island clean. But it's more random, more hit-or-miss. Wait for justice all you want, wait for the poop felons to get crap all over their gas pedals and apartment vestibules and learn their lesson, and wait and wait.

I went home, where I rinsed off my boot with the hose in front of our apartment building.

It became very clear very quickly that poop was more of a thing at the park than I had expected. It makes sense, since in the city you walk your dog and let it poop during the same trip to the park. You have to engage with the other owners on that level. There aren't many situations in everyday life where you find yourself in a group of people talking about the fine details of, in the words of comic George Carlin, "doodoo, caca, poopoo, and good old number two." Maybe when you're in fifth grade, or in a retirement home, or living with your friends from fifth grade in a retirement home; maybe not.

At Amory, I saw owners conversing daily—sometimes about big life decisions and philosophies—while holding bags of poop in their hands, sometimes clear bags in which you could spy greenish brown logs through the steamed-up plastic. (The clear bag phenomenon? File it under TMVI, too much visual information. The world never needs to see your dog's special deliveries, no matter what the size, color, or consistency.) The bags dangled and swung pendulously from people's hands as they discussed this or that owner who never picked up his dog's poop, or how their dog had loose poop today, or how your dog ate goose poop yesterday, or the fact that the garbage can was brimming with bags of poop, or which poop belonged to which dog—how, for example, those curved blond turds were recognizably the product of Dusty and not Bucky. Bucky, the hound, everyone knew, always produced miniature cow pies when he squatted, while Dusty, the cocker spaniel, daintily dropped her solids one at a time while ambling forward, hind legs bent.

Sometimes, I'd be near a person who happened upon a stray bowel movement, a voluminous and frozen still life, clearly the product of a colossus of a dog, and he or she would say they were doing a Good Samaritan "poop it forward" deed while complaining about the horrors of picking up after a strange dog. "This is SO gross!" Bagging your own baby's fresh poop was fine, and you were happy to see it; but grabbing the cold, weighty artifact of a mysterious dog was gagworthy.

Some owners, it seemed, were deeply in sync with their dogs. I included myself in that group. We'd developed a second sense about when our dog would be looking out for a spot, the exact right spot, to go. We'd instinctively glance over as the hind legs stiffened, the gait changed, the sniffing intensified, and then, voilà, the curtain lifted. It was part of the urban compact, the result of living in close quarters, that we stored our dog's bathroom schedule somewhere high in our subconscious and kept plastic bags in our pockets.

I noticed that Bertha, the golden retriever, had particularly strong privacy needs. She'd meander as far away from her owner, Nash, and the other people and dogs as she could in order to get it done. With her nose to the ground, she'd wander onto the hillside, or over behind the picnic tables— anywhere at a distance, anywhere that would pull Nash out of his world and into hers for a few minutes. This was her command performance. If Toby started to follow her as she set out, I'd call him back—"Let Bertha go in peace, Toby"—and he'd come, as if intuitively aware of her wish for time alone. For his first quarter hour of conversation at the park, Nash would be a little distracted, following Bertha's orangey outline as she moseyed away oh so slowly across the grass, her hips sashaying, savoring one of the things in her dog life that she alone could control. He never seemed to miss it, Bertha's hunkering down and the calm focus in her eyes, and he'd jog off with bag in hand, doing a poop mime for anyone who might notice. Bertha, meanwhile, would be back in the group, refreshed, before Nash had returned.

Other owners, I quickly learned, didn't like remembering poop, didn't like picking it up. They'd block it out. These people brought their dogs and then ignored them as they wandered nomadically in search of the perfect spot. These poop delinquents chatted away, forgetting their dogs' most basic purpose because they really, really wanted to tell you about last night's restaurant; they were negligent, often flaky, sometimes quite nice, and, alas, they never learned. One delinquent, Carey, always seemed to be in the middle of a long story when a more vigilant person—a self-appointed sheriff, often Margo—would inevitably yell at him across the field, "Yoo-hoo, your dog pooped!" And Carey would wave and yell back *Thank you!* with a little too much good cheer, tearing himself away from his audience to go in pursuit of Otto's shit. His words expressed appreciation, but his thought balloon read "Yoo-hoo, stop interrupting me." He proceeded to overthank the sheriff, adding, "Really, I appreciate it" as he passed by her, a shot of gratitude with a hint of bitter. He'd move toward the scene of the crime with a bag in his hand, walking slowly and looking down for long minutes in a distended poop mime that too often yielded nothing.

Dog park people ultimately forgave the poop delinquents like Carey, I saw, who were maddening but not malicious. But the poop rebels, who willfully rejected the system, who scorned the public trust, who refused to do their duty by picking up their doodie, they were reviled! They were not spacey or distracted; they were just brazen repudiators. Dog owners loved to indulge in trash talk about those people, who were so stubbornly selfish. I'd found myself listening to many antirebel tirades in only the few months I'd been going to Amory.

There were full-on interventions with poop rebels. I'd already seen a few ugly confrontations. But the rebels persisted no matter what. Interventions didn't register on them, since the rebels didn't play the social game. They didn't care about community sentiment or niceties. They breezed in and breezed out, the park serving as their dumping ground.

I saw one couple in blue down jackets have a yelling volley with Margo that first December, when she mentioned bags and offered them one. The blue down couple cursed her, and all the other Amory people, for being snobs. Their hound, who'd pooped nearby, was a good old rangy dude, friendly and grounded, but they were too defensive to follow his example. They were snubbing the snobs, who actually weren't snobs, which I think made them the snobs. It was their shit, not ours. Margo was frazzled from the interaction, getting such unadulterated hate from other dog owners; in her mind, people who own dogs should all be decent. Just like all poets and mental health gurus should be kind. She wanted to like people. The space between her eyes was in a rare furrow after the fraught interaction.

But she recovered rapidly once they left, and I'll be damned if she didn't go and clean up their dog's pile of shit anyway.

Of the poop rebels, the ideologues such as Ky were the most confusing subset. He was an organic rebel. He simply didn't like rules, any rules, because rules threatened his individuality. He wasn't lazy or elitist, like most other rebels; he just didn't want to carry society's crap around with him—literally and figuratively. He was misguided in his revolutionary and self-proclaiming fervor, as he dragged his politics of freedom into the wrong domains. He was a hippie cowboy, but leaving poop in the desert wilderness of the Old West was not like leaving poop in a town square. That was my feeling now. Had I left a few poops here and there in the area during my few weeks at the park? Yes. My secret here to tell. Would I again? No.

Not long after the December day I stepped in Trixie's shit, Ky disappeared from the park scene, one of those people who came for a few weeks or months and then move on to other parks, other colleges, other jobs, or other lovers. Our friendship was over. I realized that Margo and Nash and Noreen were steadies, and so was Saul; but others were guest stars, like on a sitcom.

I saw Ky one or two more times at the park that month before he phased out, and during our conversation I half-jokingly mentioned my run-in with Trixie's poop, but he didn't react with sympathy. He laughed and seemed to be stepping away from me as I described how I recognized her shit; he sensed I was holding him accountable, and clipping his spirit, and being a parent. I'd instantly become the inevitable authority figure, making him own his own shit. A layer of wariness fell over his brown eyes. I was that guy.

I saw him again, for the last time, in the fourteen-items-or-less line at the Cambridge Whole Foods market. It was near Christmas, and he was standing tall and wearing his Mexican hoodie, a knotted, clear bag of cold red meat in his hand. I was waiting in another lane, and I waved when he eventually gazed dully in my direction. But he didn't seem to see me, or recognize me. Ky looked through me and beyond, as if I were invisible.

caravan margo

Every time I returned to the park in the latter part of December, I felt like I was looking at a winterscape painting that was something akin to Brueghel meets Zap Comix—village activity with yellow nylon and giant knit hats and muddy boots and a pack of freaks milling around in an ice-mud-snow mix with jumping dogs. There'd be old Saul, walking slowly from group to group, one of which inevitably contained Noreen, talking, and Nash, telling his jokes, with Bertha sniffing for grass nearby. Guest stars would drift by, their dogs pulling them into conversations. Margo would be in a state of fluster. I wandered, dutifully following Toby as he proudly leaped from dog to dog and owner to owner.

It had been many weeks since I'd left Margo struggling to round up Travis after having listened to Maya's owner have a fit of dam burstage. One day between Christmas and New Year's Day, I was at the park with Toby, who was growing into a lanky boy whose eyes were beginning to smile along with his lips, and Margo was screaming to me this time, across one of the empty baseball diamonds.

She was pushing her arm out straight, bending up her right palm in the "stay" command, and yelling "Stay!" Her high-pitched voice sounded like meowing in the far distance as she yanked Travis, now on his leash, toward us with her other hand. It was a cold morning, and bits of ice crunched beneath her as she worked to keep her footing. Unless I'm more out of touch with fashion than I think, she was wearing cotton pajama bottoms again—this pair had a cartoon animal pattern—and white socks with clogs.

There were only a few other people on the field, but chilly gusts of wind were tossing the tree limbs and blowing traffic sighs over from Beacon Street, so I pretended not to hear Margo yelling. It was not a flattering moment for me, but I wasn't up for the commotion. Every time I'd seen her at Amory in the past few weeks, she'd been a swirl of turmoil. I accelerated slightly in the opposite direction, Toby's head bobbing at my right knee, his panting increasing, heading toward something good, looking up at me. She kept yanking Travis toward us, her arm out and her palm up, calling. I could feel her smiling aiming at me like a laser.

I finally stopped. Toby noticed them, ran to them, jumped at Travis, then ran back to me and looked up gamely, thinking I was going to pull a toy from my jacket pocket and throw it. His hind legs bent as he faced me, shaking with the anticipation of being chased by Travis, his eyes in their still slightly chubby sockets darting back and forth between my hands. Where's the toy? From the start, he's always had only one thing on his mind.

"Stay, stay, stay!" she said with breathless laughter at her own wit as she reached us in a slow jog, her red hair and Travis's reddish fur ears rippling in the breeze. She was ignoring Tra-vis's resistance; he was holding his neck back against her tugs like a toddler recoiling from cough syrup as she dragged him away from obsessive smacking on another dog's ball.

"It's great to see you again," she said.

And so the man who didn't know how to play wound up with a puppy who was born to play with others, who'd begun to see the world as a series of potential games. In the middle of the night, once Toby began sleeping at the end of our bed, I would reposition my body and suddenly find myself caught in a round of footsie—his warm, fuzzy paw on my bony foot, which stuck out from the sheets, then my foot on top of his paw, then his paw on top, until I fell back to sleep. He was always on the make for some clowning. I was getting a sense of the poetic justice of dog ownership, in that your dog confirms your view of the world or directly challenges it—somehow becomes your partner in the progress of your identity.

I'd begun to imagine the individual park people I'd been meeting and their respective dogs as little caravans of personal-ity, each member of the pair an ongoing, unfolding story about the other as told to those standing on the field. The variations, it seemed, were endless: The thin, insecure man and his cocky, proud poodle looked like a study in compensation; the man ambled onto the field, while the poodle charged forward. The awkward dude and his schnooky basset hound mix acted like long-lost brothers in unique stance; they puttered together. Nash and Bertha: Fred and Ginger. The depressed professor and her happy gray-blond Yorkie got out of the house, recovered balance; she wandered toward the group, while her Yorkie circled her ecstatically, urging her forward while protecting her. The newly divorced man who was looking for a fresh start, only his old, failing mutt, Maya, forced him to grieve; they stood by each other.

Empty nesters showed up at the park with misbehaving dogs who filled the gap and tapped their unused leadership; young couples parented puppies prebaby; single people let their dogs lead them to potential partners. An owner and his or her dog could become like siblings, like parent and child, like child and parent, re-creating and redoing those basic familial relationships as you might with a therapist. When I looked long enough, when I opened my gaze, I was beginning to see that we all have a fateful connection to our dogs as we create a life passage or two in tandem. We travel in caravans.

In a visual equivalent of the caravan effect, the park people also looked like their dogs, or they didn't look like their dogs at all. In twos and threes, they were an optical full rhyme, or an off rhyme, or a nonrhyme, inescapably related across a stanza. One man I met at the park was chalky and bone-thin, his knees like burls on a pair of birch trees, and he and his white greyhound, ribs detectable, hiked the park with the same delicate lope. It was a lovely and yet eerie sight, such synchronicity between species.

Toby and I had twin probosces, but our passions were at odds. I brought my glass bubble, my caution and resistance, to the park, and Toby brought a free spirit born to make friends, to entice them into tugs-of-war and ball games and dashes. That was our caravan. From the start, he was a thoroughly social animal, following Tom and me around the apartment, on the trail of collective activity. He would lie down in spots on the floor where, with a swing of his head, he could see both of us when we were in different rooms, as if to yoke us together and form a gathering in his mind. With his head swiveling on his shoulders, moving from side to side, he saw a group.

He'd bounce among our houseguests in an open plea for attention, making them bend and stretch down to him, united in a game of Twister. During my first visits to Amory Park with Toby, I could feel him pulling me into the game without knowing he was doing it, his urgency so profoundly part of his temperament. If I'd been more social, maybe I'd have been dragging him—like a guy named Gary, who loved people but explained to me during one of my first visits that his cocker spaniel, Midnight, was "not a dog person." Gary mingled, talked with other dog people, while Midnight sat quietly, a furry garden gnome, his eye on the parking lot, the car, home. But that wasn't our deal. Toby was leading me out. The leash was always tight, no slack, whenever Toby and I could see others.

I couldn't yet say exactly what Margo and Travis were working out together on that field, but I suspected it had something to do with her dreams of inner peace, her fantasy of a life without stress or the rigors of crass pop culture. If Margo could rid her mind of modern detritus, sail across the pure waters of ancient humanity on a gust of meditation, she felt she could savor every second here on Earth. Travis was supposed to help her reach nirvana, and she often would say with a smile, knowing she was repeating it again, "God spelled backward is dog."

But Travis's dreams were thoroughly terrestrial—zooming across the field after balls, stealing balls, chewing on balls, hoarding balls. He was the pleased lord of all shiny toys, and of dirty, torn-up toys, too. No wistful fellow he. As much as she wanted to let go, he wanted to happily hold on to new objects with his jaw. At the park, Margo and Travis were an ouroboros of self, as she tried to shed her ego, while he lived to feed his. The more she sought out her ideal, taking the dog into a spot of nature to commune with the trees and the people, the more he kept things earthbound and real.

"Look how cute little Toby is," she said, catching her breath, still holding Travis on his leash. "He's getting bigger and bigger." Toby was now sniffing at Travis, his moist black nose up and twitching and his tail swaying, still too young to recognize he was the object of scorn.

"He's so friendly," she gushed. "Good boy, Toby. Travis can be cranky and ball-obsessed, but he'll relax. He's not always feeling social."

"Yup," I said, nodding. In her extroversion, she couldn't see me blinking as she talked. I had this knee-jerk reaction; whenever I sensed a formation—writers, gays, college friends, dog owners—I would position myself adrift in the margins, the disconnected observer, the guy with the soft gray aura. And after decades, your heart becomes written into your physiognomy—hurt, fear, need, resignation, desire, there in the lines and contours of your face. I recall my features as angular and, in the stress of the moment, clamped down. But Margo, with her rectangular glasses, was blind to the barriers of the face, or maybe she saw through them.

She talked about the neighborhood quirks—the old houses

getting redone and the parking getting tighter. "This is great, to have outdoor space for dogs in the city," she said. "You know there are people always trying to shut us down?" She'd already talked to me about the park as a political entity—it was one of her favorite subjects—and my mind wandered to Tom and our DVR, where episodes of shows were collecting like sealed letters from friends, a pile waiting to be opened and read. Travis continued to pull at his leash.

"Anyway, I've seen you and Toby at this wacky place a lot lately," she was saying, "and I wanted to find out if you've been enjoying it."

It was a sweet burst of warmth. She laughed, I thanked her and told her yes, and we both looked down at our dogs.

Toby, now almost five months old, had just started dancing in front of Travis in a puppy fit, skedaddling left and right, catching Travis's eye with his headfirst romp. I held out a round red rubber ball, which Toby grabbed from my hand and pushed toward Travis's face. Travis stopped fighting his leash, and he was now holding himself still and watching and whining and squealing at Toby's signal to play. The ball! They were two engines revving, ready to tear up the track.

"Let's try this," Margo said, unhooking her rainbow leash from Travis's collar, hoping he wouldn't just run back to the dog whose ball he'd been stealing. "Sometimes Travis will play when it's one-on-one. He's not a fan of the group event."

And in an instant, Travis was chasing Toby and the red ball into the middle of the park, away from the parking lot and away from us. Toby's face was joyous, and yet sober with determination, with the responsibility of having to keep Travis engaged. He slipped on the little icy patches, a leg veering out of control for a second, but he kept his lead and kept the prize in his mouth. He looped around with the ball and kept running, turning his head back slightly to make sure Travis was still following. His moment was complete—the ball, the chase, the lead.

Travis reached Toby, tackled him, played-bowed slightly at him, and they began to wrestle, the ball still firmly in Toby's jaw no matter what, a bright red O. It didn't matter that Travis was bigger than Toby; they were on the same page, flopping around and rolling together, unaware of the icy snow beneath them. Watching them, I started to feel something remarkable. There's a surprising amount of satisfaction in watching two dogs at play, I've learned that over the years; but this was my first taste of that giddiness, of viewing the choreography of dog pleasure so very closely that you feel it yourself. Really, it's a physical sensation, vicarious and yet visceral. Toby and Travis had drawn us into their spell.

Staring at the dogs, Margo and I stood side by side while Toby bowed and noogied his snout into Travis's face, the ball perched at the end of his puppy bite. Toby was fearless, taking on this giant undaunted, while Travis moderated his moves for his smaller partner, going on his back and letting Toby get on top of him. They rolled over and over in place, a noodling, gymnastic wonder. The transcript of the play went something like this: "I'm the king!" "No, I'm the king!" "Okay, you're the king!" "No, you're the king!" "No, I'm the king!"

Margo and I began laughing out loud, at first in an idling giggle, but then, gradually, in a full-on laugh, our mouths open, as if we were next to each other at a stand-up comedy concert. Margo's easy posture, and the way she danced a little in her clogs as she cackled hoarsely, only made the whole show funnier. Her laugh was gutsy and loud. She knocked my arm with the back of her hand every time Toby sneaked under Travis or shook his puppy snout like a mean predator. And then I was knocking her arm, too. We were watching the crude theater of a kids' matinee, a pair of stooges doing slapstick.

The play was rough, but no skin was broken, and neither dog was exhibiting signs of fear. A self-appointed coach, Travis was pushing Toby to the limit, showing him how to get another dog riled up and engaged without getting wounded. Travis was acting like Toby's personal Stanislavski, egging him on to new levels of presence and authenticity and risk in his theatrical technique. I was touched by the way Travis, usually in a bubble of ball fixation, had automatically taken on the role of tutor, just as I was touched by almost any father-son-like bonding I saw on TV. It was the chink in my armor. Travis was helping Toby learn to play, to be daring and stay safe at the same time. I was enthralled.

The two dogs looked like a blur of red and yellow fur rolling over and over in the porthole of a clothes dryer. They seemed to be in complete physical sync, even while their actions were obviously spontaneous. To get Toby to let go of the ball, Travis would occasionally pinch Toby's loose skin with his mouth, but Toby held fast. Finally, their mouths were both locked onto the ball; the red rubber disappeared as they stared at each other face-to-face, up close and personal.

It was oddly intimate, the laughter that had erupted between Margo and me. We'd gotten a sort of contact buzz from the dogs' dance. I felt a burst of warmth toward her, and the desire to continue in the moment of play for much longer. I didn't know Margo very well at that time, but as our dogs wrestled, so compatible, I truly liked her. I wanted more of this kind of connection, so joyous and simple and from the gut. It was one of those moments when the cliché "a new world opened up" was almost justified. I understood this as the dogs began to lose interest in each other and Toby returned to me, having lost the ball to Travis, and looked up into my eyes, wondering what was next. Another ball? For me, it had been an episode of unguarded pleasure from out of nowhere, shared with a near stranger.

Margo walked out toward Travis with her leash in hand and her Chuckit tucked into her belt, and Travis started wandering away from her, ball in mouth, toward new balls on the horizon, as in the corner of his eye he saw her approach. She moved farther and farther from me as she pursued him, yelling "Stay" to him, and we parted without good-byes. I could see Saul off in the distance, doing his slow walk, looking over at the sound of her voice as she moved closer to him. I guess she assumed that Toby and I would wait for her, or that we'd be back again soon and we'd get the ball then. She was off on another chase of her own, another challenge to meet with Travis, compelled away from our little laugh riot. It was instantly clear that hellos and good-byes are not automatic or expected at the park, not by the dogs and not by the people.

In the distance, I saw Saul redirect his slow walk toward Margo, ready to draw her into a conversation, to reminisce. I put Toby on his leash to leave, but he'd quickly learned a new skill from Travis. He didn't want to quit the land of play, with its smells of cold, wet earth and snow and the pee of other dogs, so he sat, his bum like an anchor, while I tugged, his neck flexing back against the leash. Stubborn boy, getting stronger every day.

I won, and I got Toby in the backseat of the car for the ride home, his head at my elbow as he positioned himself between the two front seats, looking ahead to the next adventure. Home, okay let's go there now. He looked up at me with a sparkle in his eyes, trusting that I was now taking him someplace good. His panting was a smile. At about the time we passed out of the parking lot and onto Amory Street, I gave him a cookie for no reason—something trainer Don discouraged. "Make them earn it," he'd urged us. And then I gave Toby another cookie.

lesson learned

At that same point, as December blended into January, I decided to give up on Toby's little lesson at the park entrance. Seriously, watching Toby and Travis play together that day with Margo became a classic moment for me, because I felt the pleasure so intimately. I'd seen Toby play plenty by then, but there was something about the dance of his play with Travis, and about the dance between me and Margo, that pushed a good button.

I tried to explain it to Tom, how rigorous and perfect the dogs were in their wrestling, how Margo and I were in sync with them. "That's great," he said, happy that I'd finally started to say positive things about my experiences at the park.

Almost overnight, I no longer felt the compelling need to get Toby to sit for me upon arrival. I ceded victory in the struggle, on the grounds that he was just too cute, that he was responding well to other training efforts, and that I now had begun to understand what he was hungering for. I didn't feel that I'd lost the contest; I sensed that we were both going to win.

I recall that day of letting Toby go right off the bat as quietly pivotal, when I truly recognized my own caution and resistance and how I had been projecting it onto my dog. There was no real reason for me to detain him at that moment when we got to the park, and my compulsion to do so was starting to feel oppressive. He wanted to play; I needed to learn to play. What was the point of fighting those instincts? Aren't we often afraid of what has the power to change our lives? So now when we stepped onto the grounds of Amory, I'd immediately release Toby from the leash every time, letting him get straight to his fun. He'd tear off into the great whatever, absolute readiness. It was a small moment, but a significant moment for me, dropping the need for control for the sake of wildness. Okay, Sting; I loved Toby, so I set him free. And that set me free.

From that point on, Toby would gallop fast beyond me toward the dogs and dog people, then stop and crouch as one or two dogs in the field met him, sniffed vaguely at him, and sniffed more directly at his crotch area. He'd roll and run double time, so short and close to the ground, his bones seemingly rubber. Everyone would turn and look at him, oohs and ahs and "so cute" blowing toward me on the wind.

Our struggle had been a perfect externalization of my eternal struggle, the urge to run free and the fear of letting go. The wish, the fear. From that day on, I started relaxing into ordinary park life, finding something for myself in the off-leash world and being willing to go to the dogs. I decided that the battle was not worth fighting, that the little goose didn't need to have his exhilaration quelled to soothe my need, and I unleashed him right away. No more pushing down of the tush.

I don't think he even noticed the change in my policy. We

left the parking lot and hit the grass, and Toby flew forward, off to find some fun and some smells. Such a small instant, the unlinking of a hook. I recall it and my interaction with Margo as the moment I began to see clearly the simple satisfaction to be found in the dog park, and to become addicted. Just focus on the pleasure of the dogs at play. I started to build friendships with people, some that occasionally reached outside of Amory, some not. People formed relationships as work husbands and work wives at the office; and dog people did something like that in the mornings and evenings. And those park spousal relationships tended to be with people whose dogs were compatible with our own.

Early on, we'd met Nash and Bertha, the lovely maternal golden retriever who was like canine honey. She had a sashay of a walk, and her furry legs and butt were like a skirt over narrow tiptoe feet. Bertha was only two years older than Toby, and she quickly became his older sister, the closest thing to his mother he'd encountered since he'd left his real mother a few months earlier. If she approached Toby for the stick he was chewing on, or the tennis ball he held in his jaw, he'd instantly drop it for her, dutifully. Right away, he respected her. He knew who Bertha was. She'd pick up his stick with her teeth, enjoy it in flagrante for a few seconds, shake her head with it, then drop it a few feet away and walk off, sniffing. Toby was finding his own position in a group setting, and she was the one he looked up to first. Bertha was the fluffiest, most flirtatious little lady to us owners, but to Toby, she was a magical princess. In those first few days, they'd occasionally wrestle, and it was warming to see Bertha school the boy, who would always be a boy. She'd mouth his neck, and let him mouth hers. They'd lock mouths over a tennis ball, just as Toby had locked mouths with Travis. Toby was under Bertha's spell, and so was I. She'd push her reddish blond head into my hand, demand some scratching and petting, and I'd give it until she was done.

And I began talking more and more to her owner, who was an unshaven guy with a winky eye and a hat that had flaps down over his ears. Nash was like a comic, a Demetri Martin or a Jon Stewart, as he'd make strange connections between words and deconstruct the week's most absurd news.

Every so often, as Nash was reviewing the ridiculousness of some war, or quoting from *This Is Spinal Tap,* or extolling the miracles that are duct tape, scotch, and 1980s punk pop, Bertha would play-bow at him and bark and growl, and he would bow toward her and bark and growl back. They'd mock-threaten each other for a minute. Then she would run off, and, out of breath, Nash would return to the loose semicircle of people to bat jokes around for an hour, everyone cold and shivering simultaneously. I began to look for him, as well as for Margo, upon our arrival.

Saul had become a familiar interruption in the dog people groupings, even with winter upon us and only the more hard-core dog owners willing to brave the cold. One day, I was walking with Margo and Travis and Nash and Bertha, and we greeted Saul, and then we all began listening to him talk about how he liked walking around the park in spite of the weather. His doctor had told him to go for daily walks, and he was doing it, and, he said, the dog people were the highlight.

I could see that Margo and Nash were beginning their own conversation, a reminder to me that, at the park, it was everyone for himself. If you got stuck talking to someone you were not in the mood for, no one, not even a park spouse, was obligated to help you out. You needed to find your own way to bungee out; in terms of park morality, you're on your own, buddy. Plus, my patience regarding Saul was growing. He was so nice, and I wasn't in a rush to be anywhere. So that day, Saul and I began a chat, which he quickly brought around to his anger at a woman who was hurting his feelings. We were having a sidebar from Nash and Margo, and he fell right into it, telling me about the park walker who circled Amory every day, but who would not say hello to him. He would nod, he told me, and he would even salute to her playfully, but she refused to smile back or say hello, or even blink. It really bothered him, and seemed to undermine his well-being.

"What did I ever do to her?" he asked, outraged. He was almost shaking.

I'd seen the woman, an intense athlete now in her mid-forties, speed walking in circles around Amory. I knew exactly which woman Saul was talking about. She'd just barrel forward, with her arms marching and her earphones on, a vision in black tights. Her curly hair went up from her forehead, and her eyebrows tilted up at the ends, like Elsa Lanchester's in *The Bride of Frankenstein*. She was not particularly friendly, but it didn't bother me, because she wasn't a dog person, and she was just getting her workout. I'd certainly been prone to feeling snubbed, too easily sometimes. The older I got, though, the less I wanted to entertain those impulses. Scanning for rejection was a waste of precious time. But it really bothered Saul, for whom the idea of earbuds and podcasts and even cell phones was too futuristic. He wanted the world to be what it had been when he was an eager young man and everyone nodded on the streets and it was a small world. He was a good guy, but he'd started to forget all his years of learning about adult life, and he was vulnerable. His protective walls were crumbling, like mine, but with a different outcome.

I didn't know what to say to him, because I understood where the speed walker was coming from. A strange old guy with a dirty jacket saying hello and saluting? It could be weird. But in the next few weeks, every time I'd see that woman, so closed up, I'd want to get her to say hello to Saul. I wanted to tell her she'd make a difference in someone's life by just greeting the person and smiling.

the charlottes

That January, I was beginning to get into a rhythm, moving smoothly from my professional life in front of the TV and the computer, Toby snoozing at my feet, to morning and early-evening visits to Amory. I even felt a new and different energy seeping into my *Boston Globe* writing, since my days were now bookended by fresh air and dog play. I was still running hot and cold about having to socialize with whoever happened to be at the park, asking Saul-like questions about their dogs, but the outings were becoming part of our routine, enough so that Toby would start looking at me with some urgency every afternoon around 4:30. Nash and I began to call each other to plan a rendezvous.

And then the rhythm skipped at the tail end of January, when Toby and I got caught in a violent episode at the park. I'd seen a lot of violent scenes on TV. When they were strategically filmed, I cringed in disgust, maybe covered my eyes. But usually my heart wasn't fully engaged in the revulsion. It was just some generic *Law & Order* villain of the week or a soulless thug on *The Sopranos* or *The Sheild,* and his cruel work was a tableau of fake blood, cosmetic bruises, and, perhaps, lolling in the periphery of the image, a detached rubber finger. Tom and I would yell "Gross" and "Eww," and I would wonder what the fake blood was made of—syrup, beet juice, red dye no. 2?

But when Toby was being attacked, I did not cringe or cover my eyes. Seeing his happy puppy soul punctured by terror for the first time, fear now forever part of his emotional vocabulary, I became electric. It was adrenaline that shot through me in a fraction of a moment, a state free of self-consciousness and doubt. It was a purely physical instinct. Not for a blink did I waver as I threw my hands into the fray—a terrible idea, I know now, but my first instinct—to yank a jacked-up whippet named Sugar off of my puppy. You're better off getting another person to help you, so that each of you can grab a dog by the back feet and pull the two dogs apart, or doing something safer and more considered, but I wasn't thinking. Sugar could smell young Toby's submissiveness, his complete ignorance of predation, and she'd pounced.

I could hear Toby squealing helplessly from within the tangle as fur twined with fur and Sugar thrust her neck forward like an old-fashioned manual sewing machine. I thought I heard her teeth clattering like a box of nails. Each of Toby's shrieks tore another hole in my heart.

I'd first met Charlotte in December, and I was drawn to her literary streak. A close talker, petite, but with wide eyes, she was in my face right away about the mystery novels she secretly liked and the Victorian classics she loved and ought to be reading. As a longtime addict of heavily populated doorstop serials by Dickens and Trollope and Gaskell, the nineteenth-century equivalent of the HBO lineup, I was intrigued. She made deliberate eye contact, which caused me to want to stare back, as if hypnotized by her. She'd already put her two dogs in her car that day, but she lingered in the parking lot to talk while Toby ran onto the field with a tennis ball protruding from his jaw, head held high, a chasee advertising for a chaser. I explained that I was new to the park, and Charlotte welcomed me with her toothy smile and her boyish blond haircut. How old was this bony little lady with the piercing eye contact? I couldn't tell if she was fifty or seventy.

We talked about Trollope and the growing relevance of his themes of financial ruin and moral shiftiness. "*The Way We Live Now* is the way we still live now," she said, which made me feel as though we were a match. Not a lot of people you met at the park, or anywhere, for that matter, were interested in talking about Victorian novels, and so I was excited about the connection.

It was one of those anonymous yet friendly encounters indigenous to the dog park. I knew nothing about Charlotte except that she was a chatty chipmunk, that she took care of two dogs, and that—unlike Ky—she'd dropped a bag of poop in the barrel right before we spoke. And she knew only that I was this guy who read books and was willing to talk about them. And we clicked. You entered the park pretty much just as yourself—often there was no status jockeying up front, no immediate or obvious social hierarchy, so the connections could feel disarming. Charlotte struck me as a possible new friend. And when she told me she was a therapist—well, that fact always turned me into a willing listener. I always presumed compassion when I met a therapist, having had a really compassionate therapist in my life when I needed him. We talked more the next few times I saw her, while her dogs chased each other, disinterested in Toby, who charged around with other puppies. The chemistry grew.

On that ugly late January day, her thickset boxer mix, Thumper, was on a leash, while Sugar ran free. As we walked from the parking lot into the field together, Charlotte explained that Thumper had been attacked by another dog, so she wanted to keep him close by. Thumper resembled a thuggish gangster, with a boxer face but the paws of a bullmastiff, and toes and nails that could almost be fingers. Sugar seemed a lot more fragile. She was a white sliver of a thing, a year-old whippet who looked like she'd slide into an invisible dimension if she missed a meal. But she was packed solid with muscle, a lean, mechanical, knifelike creature with a slightly protruding backbone.

Before we got far, standing near the baseball backstop off the parking lot, I noticed Sugar standing still and staring at Toby. It was a hard stare, as if there had been an offense. And was she curling her lip and showing some teeth? Toby didn't even notice it as he jogged in circles around us, sliding over some ice, a ball sticking out of his mouth. He looked like a chunky little guy whistling happily to himself.

Then Thumper started barking and pulling against the leash Charlotte held, while Sugar stepped toward Toby and Toby stepped toward me. The weight all leaned in one direction at once. The tension had built and then built some more, all inside of a second. And in the tip of the balance, like a thunderbolt, Sugar was on Toby and at his neck, and Toby began yelping—it sounded like a car skidding with the brakes on.

I got hold of him as fast as I could, which felt like an eternity, and, shoving Sugar's tensed neck away with one hand, picked up Toby with the other, grabbing under his chest and front legs. I could feel him shaking hard and I saw a stain of blood near his throat. Sugar was jumping at me to get to Toby, her teeth bared, and I was turning in circles to dodge her. Charlotte babbled "Sug-Thump-Sug-SUGAR" but was unable to move forward to get Sugar, since she was holding Thumper back. It was as if a giant game of Mouse Trap had been set in motion. I twirled and Charlotte pulled and Sugar jumped, and there was no stopping it.

For a second, Charlotte looked like she was at the reins of a horse-drawn carriage tumbling down a mountainside, lost in the physical challenge of holding one leash while trying to grab Sugar's collar. She looked absurd in her discombobulation, as if her facial features were no longer in their usual places—her eyes tumbling from her forehead to her cheeks and her mouth askew. I was sucked into her cloud of chaos, still twirling and frowning and lifting Toby. Vaguely, I heard a few other dogs barking in the distance, out of sensory focus, like everything else around me except Toby and the vulnerable softness of his quivering body, his young bones and perfect fur.

"What happened?" I said to Charlotte, who wouldn't look at me, as the crisis passed. I don't know why I said that—it didn't matter what she'd say; I'd seen it all myself and knew what had happened. I still held Toby, though he was getting ready to get down to the ground, starting to squirm and push his legs against my arms, hungry to grow up and be independent. Sugar had been put on a leash, and a stranger was pulling her back and away.

And only then did I fully realize that we'd been surrounded, that a swarm of people had rushed over upon hearing the sounds of violence and disentangled the mess. They were an infusion of compassion. They were making sure Sugar couldn't come near us, and they were checking Toby for injury as I held him, and there was Margo in her rectangular glasses, pulling back his blond fur as if she were after mites, looking for more signs of blood.

It was a lost instant for me. When I came back to the here and now, I could see Charlotte looking miffed as the alarm subsided and the other owners stood by, a Socratic jury waiting to figure out what had happened in the Toby-Sugar shake-up. They were accustomed to Charlotte's army of defenses. She and her dogs had already caused a series of dustups, it turned out, and she was always ready with rationales and disclaimers. And she was never ready with an offer to split the veterinarian bill.

"He's okay," Charlotte stated before anyone could start dissecting the fight—it was not a question. She was in the throes of gathering her dogs' leashes, keen to avoid the inevitable slow-motion replay and group analysis, ignoring Margo's comments about how this was part of an ongoing problem. She didn't make eye contact with anyone. Nash was openly shaking his head. For a second, Charlotte was Miss Gulch. She disappeared, a twist of disarray, like a fading tornado.

———

As fast as I liked her, I didn't like her at all. It happens. I'd see her on the field in the days after the attack and she'd say hello as if nothing explosive had gone down, as if our lawyers were dealing with the problem so we could still be friends—like Simon and Garfunkel or something. So I had to do the work of mumbling hello and then wandering off like a grumbler, wondering why I wanted an apology, or an expression of concern. Was I being too sensitive? What should I do with my anger? At least she'd put her dogs on leash for a little while.

It was a negative turn, and I wanted to retreat. I couldn't bear the thought of putting Toby in the line of danger, letting him get hurt. The idea of failing him, so dependent and gleeful, sent me into a deep-seated shame spiral. An attack can just come out of the blue. And I hated seeing Charlotte and having to carry the weight of the disappointment. Margo seemed to detect my feelings, and she made me promise to come back with Toby. I could see her watery blue eyes through her black-rimmed rectangles as she pulled off a glove, asked for my cell number, and punched it into her phone. And she'd use the number if she needed to—that was her amusingly tacit threat. Even Margo, sometimes deaf to cues, knew I was still a bit tempted to choose flight over fight.

There were Charlottes at every dog park, intelligent owners who willfully resisted the truth about their dogs. In the days after the attack, I began to hear about them at length—the ones in other local parks, the ones all over the country—from various dog owners who'd heard what had happened between Sugar and Toby. The Charlottes fended off the unpleasant reality, no matter how many exasperated people explained it to them, or screamed it at them breathlessly after a dogfight; no matter how much of a therapist they were and how many couples-therapy matches they'd umpired. A Charlotte actually listened less and less the harder you yelled. It was a strangely aggressive mechanism, park denial, as it instantly weighed down those nearby, throwing unowned responsibility onto their shoulders.

The day of the attack, after Charlotte left, Margo explained to me that, in the months before I'd arrived with Toby, each time Sugar or Thumper had sprung after a dog, resulting in a jumble of ungodly wails and human screeches, levelheaded people had become more enraged; and each time, Charlotte had become more convinced she was being mistreated and ganged up on.

"She once said she felt like she was back in high school," Margo said, "but I say she's the real mean girl."

Charlotte was able to dissect each violent event in such a way that her dogs were never the instigators. "Sugar was just trying to say hello and [fill in the blank] didn't like it," or "Thumper doesn't like it when other dogs have squeaky toys." Somehow, she'd use the situation to support her need to be in the right. I could see her caravan trick—Charlotte, Thumper, and Sugar, the denial train. In one hot moment, Margo told me, Charlotte had yelled at some traumatized owner, "Show. Me. The. Blood." She couldn't hear herself. As if blood is the only proof of aggression.

And so the other dog owners at Amory, burdened with Charlotte's unaccountability, were always on the lookout as she, Sugar, and Thumper walked around the field like an incipient storm system. With Sugar's attack on Toby, I was now on the lookout, too.

At points in her park life, Margo said, Charlotte had gone through the motions of correction, token acknowledgment that she wasn't entirely blind to the situation. That was how Sugar had come to be part of her motley crew: After Thumper had bitten a large black poodle, Charlotte's solution was to get him a friend, since loneliness was surely leading him to desperate acts. It was like giving Bonnie to Clyde. The two dogs became a team, egging each other into belligerence. By the time I crossed her path, she was trying to keep at least one dog on leash at the park; although, as it turned out, that was only half a solution, which was equal to no solution. She just couldn't get with the basic fact that she owned her two dogs, no matter who those dogs were.

I saw how some owners kept their dogs on leashes every day at the park because they'd accepted that their dogs were not trustworthy around other dogs, or people, or kids. They still came, they used the park, and so did their dogs, despite some frustration; but they were in the game, playing fair. These owners were quiet heroes, I began to realize—to others and especially to those others' dogs—as they stood around talking. No dog was perfect, not just the fighters but also the poop eaters, the barkers, the beggars, and the humpers. The owners had to deal with it. What would Toby's imperfection be? I couldn't tell yet. But I knew there would be something I'd have to deal with.

Socially, Charlotte survived on a diet of fresh blood, Margo explained. Charlotte would spy a new person with a dog and latch on quickly, then drift off just as quickly after the inevitable incident. She was like a siren of the dog park, luring inexperienced sailors onto the rocks.

It was too sad, Margo said: With the most basic shift in understanding, Charlotte could have had the sweetly chatty daily community she wanted, on her side, her two dogs a group endeavor in patience and understanding. Sometimes, everyone tried to help a fearful or aggressive dog as much as they could, inspired by the owner's efforts.

I could see the way people worked to listen to Saul, despite his nostalgia and his repetitions; there was a communal endeavor to be kind to the old guy with the flipped-up sunglasses, no matter how many times he asked you the same questions.

the chewy project

I didn't need to take Toby to the vet or to Angell Memorial Animal Medical Center after Sugar's attack. The blood I'd seen on him must have been from Sugar's mouth—perhaps her gums were bleeding. I couldn't find any breaks in Toby's skin, and, more important, his spirit was undaunted. The next time we pulled into Amory, Toby was as hyped as ever, beside himself and squealing in the backseat of the car. My spirit was on alert, but with a newfound appreciation for the dog owners who'd helped us out after the attack. It was unforgettable, the support I'd gotten.

Someone suggested I call Officer Marv to register a complaint against Charlotte, but, well: Officer Marv? From the first time I saw him scouting the park for dogs off-leash after 1:00 P.M., I could tell he was not simpatico.

That February, the same kind of group undertaking to help Saul was beginning to happen with a rescue dog named Chewy, who was skittish. A midsize white dog with black lips, she was all indiscriminate nervous reactivity. She would duck her head and run when you moved your arm or reached out, even if you had a big, luscious cookie in your hand. She was flinchy and wary. So many rescue dogs arrived with rumored stories of abuse; I could tell that Chewy was the real thing—fear born of experience, a hand coming at her, or a foot, or a broom, or a bat. It's never comfortable to see yourself causing a dog to cower as you go to pet her and look in her eyes and she shrinks back in fear. It's stunning how much people and ugly twists of fate can injure and scar the heart of an innocent.

Her new owner, Stan, would linger behind the other people and dogs, there for Chewy when she backed away after her tentative explorations. I found myself walking with him a few times as we discovered the ways of the park together. He told me that he, too, had initially been turned off by the strangeness of the ad hoc park community and the obligation to socialize, and yet he was also becoming drawn to it, and not just for Chewy's sake. I felt as though we were a like pair of newcomers, but with radically different dog situations, since Toby was a picture of unfettered puppiness. He'd led a charmed life so far.

"Noreen drove me nuts at first," Stan said about the talky park regular, "and then I started liking her. She has a huge heart under all that minutiae. You just have to wait to see it. I'm glad she has this place." We were in sync.

I warned him about Charlotte, whose dogs would surely undo any progress Chewy was making if they attacked her. Oddly, Chewy had already met Sugar and Thumper, and they hadn't bothered with her; dog chemistry, and the reasons a dog bullies some and not others, is as complicated as people chemistry. Perhaps Charlotte's dogs could smell the ways of the street about Chewy, whose fears were not directed at other dogs so much as at people, and they had steered clear; perhaps it was just a mood thing, or the air pressure, or the positioning of the stars.

In his thirties, with short blond hair and a major chin dimple, Stan told me about how he'd just gotten Chewy, who was a few years old, and how she was a shy beauty. When he had her washed after getting her from an area shelter, he said, she had instantly turned from gray to white. He wasn't sure about the circumstances of her early life, but her spirit had definitely survived; you could see that just by her vigorous body wags and her tiptoe dancing. She kept her body low, with her ears back, but she nonetheless shimmied with excitement. She still wanted to connect with people, as she approached dog owners from behind them and beside them, but she had a guarded reflex—her fear was at the level of instinct. The moment you acknowledged her, she'd back off. So Stan would hang behind alone and be there for her after her forays into the group, spoiling her with cookies to help her feel pleasure and inspire her to trust him. He was the only person she would take a treat from, the only one who didn't worry her. Stan was committed to acting as her net, and exploring his own ability to care. Their caravan was a mutual lesson in nurture and safety—an equation that ended with an even number. He told as many people as he could about his efforts, and it was becoming a park-wide project to help Chewy feel at home.

No one made it easier for Chewy than Noreen. It was obvious. She had a great focus when it came to getting on a dog's level, the dog's-eye view. She could talk a lot to people, but she always acknowledged the dog, too. I'd spot Noreen on the field, and, waving, she'd yell to me, "HEY, MATT!" And then she'd call out, "Hey, Tobias J. Dog," or "Hey, Tobias J. Lab." She was a kind of acid test for anyone who showed up between eight and ten in the morning and heard her doing stand-up and making god-awful puns while her Border collie mix waited patiently at her feet. If you couldn't hack Noreen, I began to realize as the months passed, then you were thin-skinned. You can't love only the perfect dogs with shiny coats who never bark. Who wants to, when there are Chewys everywhere? Noreen was always the one who'd ask about your dog if he or she had been injured or sick; she was the one who remembered their birth dates.

Noreen would mention Chewy's name when Chewy was off exploring, sniffing quietly, but Chewy could hear it: "Look at CHEWY over there." Maybe her clear eyes would lift a touch at the sound of her name. Then Noreen would continue on her narrative about, maybe, *Carnivale,* an obscure HBO series with some die-hard fans. "So, Matt, do you think they should have renewed it?" But the point was made, and Chewy got it.

After the ninth or tenth time I met Noreen, and she talked over me with her fangirl excitement, thrilled to know that I, too, loved TV, I knew I could connect with her. With the spark in her eye, she was an unstoppable force. Being honest with myself, I had to admit that there was a little Noreen hiding inside of me, wanting attention, wanting to talk off the top of my head, fast and loud.

But Charlotte couldn't take any group support. She fought like her dogs, a small, fiery pack of unbridled persecution. She didn't ask for help, and she didn't want help. She didn't step up. Metaphorically, if not literally, she casually let the other people on the field step in shit. She chose to ignore the fact that she lived in a world with people who tread the same ground that she did.

But there was a rescue mission riding in her troubled wake, owners who found a way to step in and help out. They'd been there for me. In the coming weeks, I would look back at what had happened during the first attack, and it would reach me— the embrace of dog-park concern.

Lucinda, the owner of the Great Dane named Nellie, told me a week or two after the attack about having lost her daughter to cancer a few years earlier. She wanted to tell me that she remembered the way some of the park people had responded, with the kind of sympathy and cautious comfort that she'd needed, none of the more complicated political shtick and jock-eying that always surfaces among family and friends around tragedy. Death out of season has a way of attracting death group-ies, those looking to borrow drama, but the park people avoided that. They brought food, walked her dog, stayed nearby—not too close, but always available. People she liked, people she didn't like, people she knew well and even near strangers— they all did something kind but not overbearing.

Lucinda recalled opening her front door and seeing Drew, an athletic guy who threw a ball every day for his ridgeback mix and who'd probably never boiled an egg, standing there wearing a pair of oven mitts and carrying a heated-up frozen pizza. It was a moving sight.

Lucinda actually told me her story twice, each time with the same feeling, the same misty-eyed fondness. Years after her loss, she still seemed to find it consoling. She told me that the pack, despite internal issues, could be rabid when it came to protecting its most vulnerable members.

And she was right. The park people had been all over Toby and me that day, like a triage team, tending to and fixing what had just broken in a snap. And that's what I came to see about the Charlottes: They'd never allowed themselves that rush of protection, that social organism attaching to them like a blanket and sheltering them for a minute. They'd set up lone camp in the land of renunciation and refusal. I had a little Charlotte in me, not toward dogs, but toward the people attached to them. I wasn't always open to comfort and relief. There was a park interconnectedness that the Charlottes missed entirely, of family, of blood. I was beginning to see it.

dogs are dummies

When we'd arrive, I'd look for Charlotte, in order to avoid her and make sure her dogs were leashed, and I'd look for any potential Charlottes with threatening dogs. I'd look for Nash and Margo, for some jokes and conversations about the news and/or the universe; and Toby would search out Bertha and jump at her neck, then try to run off after the forever-in-motion Travis, panting. He loved Bertha consistently, while he seemed to have affairs with other dogs that would last only a month or a week or even just a day. One day, he was romping with Boomer, the lovely cocker spaniel, the next—and you're name is? Was my little goose going to be a lover boy with the other dogs? There were always strangers and their dogs about, too, in town for a doctor's appointment or to visit their kids. Toby's and my days were revolving more and more around our visits to Amory, and when Toby looked at me with the park spark in his eyes, I began to look back at him with the same anticipation.

I could hardly complain about sitting at my desk, and in front of the computer and the TV, chasing a deadline all day long while little Toby slept under a chair, or at my feet, or across my feet. It was a happy work situation, writing for a major newspaper about a subject that inspired me, and inspired lots of e-mail interaction with readers. No matter what I wrote about a TV show, I heard from TV lovers about it—positive and negative—in flurries of e-mail, in comments on stories, and, even, sometimes, by phone. For years, I received weekly voice messages at night from a guy who called me "Matty," who loved *American Idol,* and who shared his feelings about the failing state of American culture, his past as a radio station employee, his troubled sleeping patterns, his jobs in construction, and his asthma. I'd never met him, never spoken to him live on the phone, and probably never would. He'd hadn't mentioned his name, so my *Globe* colleague Sarah Rodman— who also got late-night calls from him—and I decided to name him Gus. We loved hearing from Gus, even when he was cranky. I'd go on the radio to talk about the latest batch of new series, or about cable TV's run on quality, or the power of violence in prime time, and I'd feel satisfied when listeners reached out to me to take issue with my choices and observations. I liked the contact.

But there was an unreality about my days that a dose of the park remedied. And I could see that other dog owners were also finding some kind of antidote at the park, something that involved the presence and attention and freedom they weren't getting from their jobs or families. You needed to watch out for your dog, to gauge the intensity of play to make sure no one would get hurt; you needed to watch for poop; you needed to assess the other owners to make sure they weren't Charlottes. You needed to listen to Noreen amid the barking. You needed to stay in the time and the place, just as the dogs did. After a few months of pushing myself to take Toby there, I was leaving my office and going more and more readily. I began to understand that these daily treks were an opportunity to let go of a few things, grab on to a few others. I had a chance to push myself to be a less anxious and removed person. And Toby got a bigger play area, with more friends and more challenges and more chasing.

Each time we went to the park, I felt as though I could see Toby growing up, growing more comfortable within a social pack. For a while, he'd stay near me in case he needed my assistance with a bigger dog; now he was less tethered. He and I were getting tight, and we had a triangular lovefest going with Tom at home, as Tom and I chased him and let him come up on the couch, where he would perch, with eyes gently squinted and his mouth hanging open; we were a trusting unit. I'd watch him and laugh at his transparency, at how easy it was to read his mind as he plotted to get another cookie or to get me to run after him. He was an open book. And my laughter fed his confidence. But I could tell that Toby was getting a validation and self-assurance from the dogs that he could never get from humans. He started to develop a strut, a pop to his step, which intensified whenever he detected another dog nearby.

There was another short chapter in my conflict with Charlotte, by the way, just as I thought I could begin to stop worrying about a Sugar attack. In February, after a snowstorm, she saw Toby and me walking the periphery of the Amory field with Nash and Bertha. Toby and Bertha had been jumping around in the fresh snow, looking like a pod of dolphins as they leaped across the white. The sight of dogs sending new powder flying, digging and romping, was a happy one; but now we were all back on the tamped-down path, lost in conversation. Charlotte had Sugar on a leash and Thumper was nowhere to be seen—probably in her car. She was crossing the width of the snowy field, heading directly toward us, moving rapidly, waving an arm, as we kept to the hill by the tennis courts, on the opposite side of the park from the parking lot. "What is she doing?" I said to Nash.

It looked as though Sugar was towing her, a sleek white skiff with a one-hundred-horsepower motor driving ahead of a small woman in a knit hat who was running too fast and whipping up flying snow like a water-skier. And just as Charlotte yelled to us, "I've got her in training, and I just want to try this again," and I yelled back, "I'm not comfortable with it," Sugar started running extra hard and pulled little Charlotte right off her feet. Charlotte landed facedown in the powder as Sugar kept rushing forward, now about ten feet from us.

Toby had moved behind us in fear, whimpering, and Nash picked him up off the ground just as Sugar got to us; I jumped toward Sugar—on Sugar, in fact. We were a mess of conflict, with me getting shivers of snow up in all those places you don't want snow to go, into my sleeves and down my neck and on my belly. But when I stood up, Sugar's collar was firmly in my hand, and I pulled her leash up from the snow. She was still trying to get at Toby, hungering for his neck, but her scampering legs were only digging down to the ground as I held her in place. "Sugar!" I yelled at the frenzied dog, but she was deaf to anything but the sound of Toby's pulse.

And then, once again in a flash, Charlotte had taken Sugar's leash from me and was gone, heaving Sugar off across the park, without an inquiry or an apology. Again she drifted away, ruffled and impenitent, snowy and cold, to that place where the Charlottes go to lick their wounds.

A day or two later, Margo reasserted her insistence that I not flee based on Charlotte's wrongheadedness.

"Travis will miss Toby if he doesn't come back," she said with a warm smirk, teasing me about my wariness. I was learning that if you wanted to say something to someone standing near you at the park, you could easily say it through your dog. And then I responded, "Travis is such a nice guide for Toby." And then Margo said, "They are a real pair."

Translation: "I like you." "I like you, too." "We should be friends."

After the last Charlotte incident, when Charlotte and Sugar would pass me and Toby in the parking lot face-to-face and I felt I should say something, I'd observe, "She doesn't seem to mind the leash." Translation: "Are you taking responsibility yet?" And Charlotte would smile and say, "She loves her trainer." She really meant "I'll humor you." Then she'd say, "Toby looks happy." Translation: "How's your coddled dog?"

We owners were speaking to one another, and somehow the dogs were serving as our language, or as our ventriloquist dummies, as if we were children putting words and emotions in the mouths of dolls while we played with them. Oh, there may have been truth there—based on Travis's facial expressions and his posture, for example, I think he really did enjoy serving as

Toby's mentor, and so did Bertha—but there was a dollop of fudge, too, a spoonful of human. We were speaking about ourselves in a way, forwarding our own thoughts and feelings by projecting them through the dogs.

Most of the time, it seemed, we didn't quite know we were doing it—it was so common at the park, and in the world of dogs. Dog ventriloquism just wended into and out of conversation like weather predictions, or descriptions of favorite foods, just another subject among many. Sooner or later, I could see that everyone at the park—all ages, all types—would try to explain the dogs' behavior and end up projecting their own interpretations. It was unavoidable. I don't care how rational or scientific an owner was, the person inevitably wound up painting his or her own words and feelings onto the dogs at the park—that the dogs were having fun, that they were bored, that Elmo and Roscoe were best friends, that Spoof and Stomp were in love.

That winter, I found myself talking a lot to Hayley, a graduate student in anthropology with thick, frizzy brown hair, a gutsy laugh, dimples on her cheeks, and a Bernese mountain dog named Stewie, after the matricidal infant in the cartoon TV series *Family Guy*. She spoke my TV language perfectly. In their caravan, Hayley and Stewie were two of a kind—tall, big presences, varying shades of brown, eager to bring a smile, not apt to bark unless provoked, but then watch out. Hayley had a stoic surface; there was nothing warm and fuzzy about her as she moved between her Boston University seminars, the tapas restaurant where she worked part-time, and the park. But she was always gunning for a laugh.

She had me on the floor when she talked about how she desperately wanted to get a new tattoo—of Margo's sweet face, her rectangular glasses, and her fire red hair. "I want to commit to that," she said, laughing about how thoroughly lovable Margo was, and how kooky she was, too.

Hayley saw me trip over Toby one day as he ran through my legs. As I quickly rolled over, stood, and dusted myself off, flustered but unhurt, I saw and heard her laughing hysterically a few feet behind me, a deep body laugh. I had to laugh with her. She told me she was going to remember me and my tumble whenever she was in need of a something to smile about. "That one is lodged in my memory bank for further use," she said.

One Sunday in late February, the Amory field covered in a much tromped-down layer of snow, Hayley and I stood talking, when all of a sudden Stewie was targeted by a German shepherd, who tore a small chunk from his ass. In a moment, the snow looked like it had a giant red kiss on it. We all pulled the dogs apart—a large rescue crew, including Margo, Nash, and Noreen—and Hayley quickly held a glove against his wound, loudly referring to the shepherd's aloof owner as an "asshole." Angry about having his day disrupted, the bald, middle-aged shepherd owner, who was wearing loafers, had literally kicked his dog away from Stewie, grabbed his collar, leashed him, and dragged him to his truck. He didn't offer money or compassion or even eye contact; after an apologetic mumble in Hayley's direction—"Sorry 'bout that"—he was gone. A Charlotte, he probably moved from park to park, putting new dogs at risk without solving the problem.

The people who'd gathered around Hayley and Stewie wanted to help, but she quickly led Stewie to her car and drove him off to Angell Memorial Animal Medical Center in nearby Jamaica Plain. I'd offered to go with, but she preferred to go alone, probably not wanting me to see her fall apart a little bit. At the park, Hayley held her shield up and kept riding forward on her own. The next time I saw her, a few days later, she said that Stewie was just fine, and so was his stitched-up butt.

"How you feeling, buddy?" I said to Stewie as he rubbed against my legs and I saw a bandage on his backside.

"I'm gonna make it after all," Hayley said back in her creaky, lovable Stewie voice.

I noticed, with affection, that Hayley happily and openly expressed herself through Stewie. "He's saying 'Come and get me,'" she'd narrate as the giant Stewie did a rocking jog in a loop around a group of owners who were kicking around a bunch of small talk. "He's saying 'You know you want me,'" she'd playfully continue, speaking to no one in particular, as if she were providing movie subtitles or sports commentary to a small crowd. Her voice would get a little higher than usual. "Look at Stewie run! He's looking for a partner in crime. Toby, play with Stewie! He says, 'You're all a bunch of lazy asses if you don't want a piece of me!'"

In her voice-over, you could hear her inviting the other dog owners to some one-on-one time with her, looking for conversation amid the chatter. She loved to engage. Hayley would kiss Stewie's white snout, scratch his back while his white-brown-black tail swung back and forth lazily, and then turn to me with a question about TV, or a joke about the stumpy Officer Marv and his rampage of harassing dog owners. She'd always had dogs, and she was used to the park culture.

Sooner or later, Hayley expressed her opinions of other people via Stewie. She was a self-aware, witty woman, and she was also a girl with a hand puppet. She had Stewie madly in love with one dog but not another, based on her own preferences toward the owners. When Hayley was turned off by someone, she'd say that Stewie, too, seemed unenthusiastic about making contact: "I don't know why Stewie seems afraid of Prince," or "Stewie's feeling shy today—sorry." You could gauge her daily state of mind by her interpretations, as she Rorschach-tested her way among the assembled few. If she didn't like a newcomer, say, a woman with a bad dye job and a frenetic vizsla whom she couldn't control, the dog scooting like a rubbery torpedo around and into people's legs, Hayley would mention something to me about how Stewie was not liking the dog. "He's getting ookie around that vizsla, I can tell," she'd say, and maybe step back and put Stewie on a leash, much to his bafflement.

Stewie always loved Toby, which pleased me, since I liked Hayley; however, sometimes Stewie was impatient with my reticent manner. "Stewie wants to play; that's why he's jumping on you," she'd explain to me, as if I were thick, as Stewie left streaks of icy wetness on my jacket.

When I started hearing couples talking about their dogs before we got Toby, I felt sure that Tom and I would never be a couple—*that* couple—who would speak to each other via their dog, the way you see in *New Yorker* cartoons. Now, I'd begun to notice our coupled friends voicing opinions that way. The communication via dog seemed inevitable. It may be easier to fall into this behavior with dogs than with kids, because at some point your kids can speak for themselves. Dogs can't talk—one more reason to love them, but also an added enticement to use them as dummies.

"Chipper has to go out," our friend Sarah said when Tom and I were having dinner with her and Brendan at their house. Chipper looked up at her at the mention of his name. "No, I don't think he does," Brendan responded as Chipper, a black Lab mix, turned his head to Brendan. "It's your turn," Sarah reminded Brendan, "because I've been with him all day." "Okay, I get it," Brendan said. We all got it. There was a little triangular volley between the couple and their dog as Tom and I sat watching, a tense little refresher course on the division of family duties. Chipper was the conduit for their mild strain that night.

Alas, it didn't take long for Tom and I to start talking through Toby. "'Gee, Tom,'" Tom would say in his Toby voice as their required evening walk approached, particularly if it was raining, "'I wish Matthew would take me for my walk tonight. I sure like him.'" I did not succumb to the guilt, but I understood Tom's message: Don't want to go outside. Or Tom would say, "Toby, did you tell Matthew that we're supposed to leave at seven on the nose?" Loud and clear.

And I found myself sending posts to Tom through Toby.

"Toby loves playing Frisbee with you; I can tell," which meant, "Play with him more, please, and tire him out." Or, when Tom wanted a quiet night, I'd say, "Toby loves being around people," meaning, "Let's invite some friends over for dinner."

It was crazy, of course, and shameless. The tangle of self and dog was intimate, psychodynamic, and pleasingly neurotic. Some people developed actual voices for their dogs, just as they'd translate their dogs' actions and facial movements into human traits. I'd begun to channel Toby's voice, and it was a low southern drawl, like the one Billy Bob Thornton in the movie *Sling Blade* had as he sat on a porch pondering life. It emerged organically. The more I explored Toby's voice, I noticed it had a philosophical tone as he responded to my comments. "Well, I wouldn't be getting too upset about that, May-thyoo," he might say to me after I'd done something stupid, a calm, consoling vote for sanity. I liked turning him into my personal—and sometimes paternal—Zen man; it was as healing as it was absurd. Toby was four or five months old, but he was leading me to treat myself and others with more kindness. " 'I think he means well, May-thyoo,' " I'd say in his voice when Tom was irking me.

Sometimes when it was just me with Toby for hours at a time, at my desk or watching TV, I'd continually free-form his thoughts aloud. "You're a lazy goose," I might say to him. "I ain't no lazy goose," he might reply in that southern voice, "but I can be a little goosey every now and then." It was sticky sweet—I completely knew that—and yet it went on all day long, each time with more conviction. Lord knows what our downstairs neighbors made of it, if they ever heard me through the floor or in the echoes of the stairwell. I'd say Toby was a goose, he'd respond, I'd say it again, and he'd respond again. I'd tell him I was an idiot for loving a bad TV show, or for saying something offensive to a friend, or for forgetting to pay a parking ticket, and he'd tell me, "You ain't so bad, May-thyoo." Throughout, Toby—the real Toby—would look at me with his tolerant brown puppy eyes, bored but potentially interested. As I kept our exchange going, the story of my inner life unraveled before his willing gaze.

Eventually, I got to the point where my ventriloquism had become something of a tic. "He's so cute," some stranger at the park observed, the steam from the cold coming out of her mouth as she looked warmly at Toby. Not thinking, I said back in Toby's drawl, " 'Why thank you, ma'am, that's awfully kind of you.' " From within her furry hood, that stranger at the park turned her head to me with an expression of absent bemusement. Is this person living in a child's fantasy world, Mister Rogers gone rogue? I saw the thought pass over her face, and I kind of didn't care.

I'd lost sight of the border—the line across which you appear too dog-obsessed—and it wasn't unpleasant. I was becoming a crazy park person. Hayley did Stewie's voice, of course, and the more Hayley and I talked at the park, the more we had Toby and Stewie talking to each other, too. It became a sick little circus.

" 'Why, Stewie,' " Toby would say, " 'I do believe you're looking a little bit malnourished today, mmn-hmm." And in his voice, Stewie would say, " 'Why, yessir, I do believe your friend Matthew needs to give me more treats.' " And then Toby would say, "'Why, I think you are a genius.'" It was childish, and that was good.

By February, I was having Toby say to me, in front of Tom, "'I know you're lazy, May-thyoo, but I need to git to the park.'"

And Tom would smile directly at me and say, "Come on, you're going for you, too." He knew that I was now getting as much from the park as Toby was. It was true. So I wasn't just going for altruistic reasons, and Tom needed to make that clear. I liked going every day, and I was not getting extra relationship points for it.

"'I could stay right here at home and play with you and Tom,'" Tom would have Toby say in response. Tom was feeling a little left out. It was a new adventure for me; for him, it was separate. I was talking a lot about people and dogs he didn't know.

It must be a twist when you marry a guy who is a bit of an introvert and then he begins to open up to a new group of people. It was one of the first divides in our coupling—not a bad break, but potentially threatening. It was one of those moments in a long-term relationship when an adjustment needed to be made—on both sides. And we were beginning that process.

"'I need to get to the park NOW,'" I'd have Toby say to me, and Tom would flinch a little.

the dog nazis

I did tend to go on and on about park life to Tom. Letting Toby loose, and the sight of Toby letting loose, was a happy drug as I watched him wrestle with other puppies and get schooled by older dogs like Travis and Bertha. With a ridiculous grin on my face, I'd stand gazing as Toby dodged and darted, my little star halfback. I was still vaguely thinking about Cesar Millan, about being the alpha, about the incantations of training—"sit," "down," "stay," "sit," "down," "stay." But the real satisfaction, the deep pleasure that jumped like sparks from my spine to my soul, was coming from the rough-and-tumble of the dogs, the leaping and rolling and mock bullying, the dancing with no steps. It was just dog play, something small, something I'd once disregarded, but I had become enthralled.

Standing next to another owner, watching our animals free-form, swimming and writhing together across the grass in some kind of primal body ballet, I felt immediacy and connection. I'd had that feeling standing that day with Margo, laughing out loud, hitting each other in the arm, and I'd had it with a

few other owners since then—the awareness that the world
and TV and my phone could wait while a pair or more of dogs
found ecstasy. Watching dogs cavort together had quickly become the gold standard of dog-park experiences. I guess it's
always like that; Watching someone you love enjoy himself becomes peak enjoyment.

And because the dogs played, the people played, too, if you
were lucky. The dogs' gravity-defying gymnastics made you
feel buoyant, in the same way good blues guitar could reach
into your chest and shoulders and make you rock. It was an
atmospheric directive. Nash was ready every morning to bat
around jokes and double entendres while the dogs did their
thing. In a down jacket and a hat with earflaps, he was like a
hit of dark-roasted coffee. He was as off-leash as Bertha. He'd
casually make bad puns, then spring-load them with meta-
commentary about how bad they were, hoping to receive a
better comeback. When he was in top form, the park was his
improv session. He became part of the bridge Toby was building to help me interact with other people, the kind of friend I
could have while exploring the ever-shifting group disposition;
he was always there in the background with his politically in-
correct narrative. He was terminally ironic, except when it
came to his sweet eye contact with Bertha—that was where
you could clearly see all his sloppy love churning. Bertha would
bow toward him and growl and he'd growl back at her, her
love slave, or she'd stroll off on a long journey to find her poop
spot and he'd trail after her like a willing dupe.

It wasn't long before Nash was mixing in the gay jokes, using
them, as some sitcoms do, as a signal of comfort and affection.
That always pleased me—when a straight person could make a

gay joke in my presence without fearing a misstep. Everyone seemed to have a designated person or two at the park with whom they'd bonded in a special way, like having a buddy when you swam at summer camp. I was thinking that Nash, Margo, and now Hayley were becoming mine.

Soon enough, it was clear to me that the Charlottes were only part of the equation when it came to taking responsibility for your dog. There was a couple who showed up at Amory every morning in a minivan, their three Belgian sheepdogs and a yellow Lab sitting still in the back like polite grammar school kids. The man and woman were all business as they unloaded their arsenal of sporting equipment, including orange neon posts, cloth Frisbees, and a stopwatch. She was stocky and aloof, and so was he. They didn't stroll and mingle with their dogs; they led them to their duties. It was like they were all going to work for the day as the couple set up the Day-Glo markers and lined up the dogs, then had them running for Frisbees in succession. There was a mathematic rhythm to their system, which formed the geometric shapes of a giant game of cat's cradle. The couple yelled out commands in French, in honor of three of the dogs, and the dogs loped back and forth and diagonally in order. And the Lab, Willie, tried to be a good boy, although he took the most grief for missing cues.

The couple was not friendly. I'd walk by them and nod, as would others, and they never responded. They were in their zone. Lord knows what Saul made of them; they made the *Bride of Frankenstein* lady look like a sweetheart. They'd stake out a corner of the field, and people would honor their wishes, doing their best not to intrude on the training camp. Paraphernalia, including metal collars and knotted rope leashes, sat at the couple's feet in the snow. "They're the dog Nazis," Nash said one day as we skirted their territory. "We should liberate those dogs." To be fair, the couple probably took pleasure in the routine; and the dogs, too, probably liked having a regular job. Despite the absence of smiles, there was synchronicity and vigor in the air as the couple flung and flicked and the sheepdogs and Lab chased and caught. Everyone had a job, which is satisfying to most dogs. But there was an obligatory feel to their workouts as they went through the same paces every day, so separate from the rest of the world. It was hard to imagine what all the rigidity was for, what the final goal was—maybe local dog shows and contests, maybe just giving them all a reason to get up and out of the house. I couldn't begin to comprehend their caravan.

One day, I was walking with Margo and Nash, and we passed by the training camp. We felt illicit, like we should be whispering along the border as we talked about this and that. Without our realizing it, Travis had crossed the line into their area and was screwing up the tightly run organization. As we heard the couple yelling to us in the distance, we saw that Travis was peeing in a long, heavy stream onto one of their posts. Dripping wet, the little plastic tower began to reflect the sun.

For the first time, we heard their American-accented voices. They shouted, "Could you get your dog?" Margo hurried over and tried to round up Travis, but the damage was done. He'd doused the marker, then moved on, running off with his long ears swaying. The guy half-yelled into the wind, "Get control of your dog," the cold making his breath visible, but then they all fell back in their mechanical groove, the Frisbees flying, the arms bending.

Soon after that, their Willie came over to Toby and me as we walked around the park. Suddenly, another yellow Lab was riding in our wake, and he had a sweet grin on his face and a light in his eyes as he reached us. He was taller than Toby, and older. He and Toby romped together for a moment, a pair of happy broncos, tongues hanging out, and I said, "Hey, buddy." I held out a dog cookie and he was taking it from me when I heard "Hey, *hey*!" in the background. It was Mr. Dog Nazi. There had been an escape. The guy was running toward us, waving his hands, objecting, I think, to the cookie I'd given his dog. Willie stood savoring his last moment of freedom, his recess, with me.

Seconds before the guy arrived with a leash, eager to hook up and walk away with his prisoner, I pulled out another cookie. Willie took it gingerly and gratefully from my side and ran off.

There was such a thing as taking too much ownership of your dog, being overly responsible; that was what the Dog Nazis made me think. We both needed to get out and sniff around, owner and dog, and play some, too. Both ends had to detach from the leash. If you had a problematic dog, or if you were a Charlotte, the process was more complicated, of course; but for me, letting Toby be free was becoming a critical part of the thrill of dog ownership. Park time was when he could let go of structure and play with others or play alone or play with me, or not play—all of which was play.

. Control was no longer feeling like the goal of this dog endeavor for me. The training, the commands, the work, the Cesar Millan protocol—they were all demoted to a much lower tier of priority. They were becoming the context, the architecture, of dog ownership. Play was the real target, to watch Toby swagger inside of the lines like a furry acrobat. Ad-libbing, letting it happen, that was what I was now enjoying, and I would cringe when watching uptight owners pull their dogs away from happy play because they wrongly feared it was too rough. I was shedding the drive to make Toby a strictly behaved dog, Tom's and my picture-perfect yellow goose, a poster boy for "the Dog Whisperer."

The Dog Nazis restrained their own team, made the dogs run on time; Officer Marv exerted his will on all Amory dog owners. He was in love with harassing and berating us. It was his passion, not just his job, to enforce the local Amory law—no off-leash dogs after 1:00 P.M. He'd get his rocks off during the afternoon, lecturing offenders about the 1:00 P.M. rule and the reasoning behind it until they were ready to beg for a ticket— anything to shut him up. And then he'd appear at the park again after hours, in civilian clothes and driving his own Chevy, to bust the unawares. Off the clock and yet still horny to hassle. Whoever first coined the word *killjoy,* thank you.

He was a stubby guy, Officer Marv, and he didn't like to get out of his car. One February morning, I was sitting at a wooden picnic table, with Toby lounging on the tabletop like a centerfold, absolutely savoring the position of height and power. We were both content, getting warmed by the sun, Toby off-leash and yet staying close to me. On his side, leaning on his shoulder, with his belly and ding-dong visible and his hind legs crossed, Toby was sighing like he'd just eaten the dinner of a king. And then along came Officer Marv in his cruiser, riding up to us over the walking path and the delicate grass, his tires tearing up the sod. His window came down.

"Do you have children?" he asked me, ignoring the one or two other people nearby. His head was a giant thumb and he seemed to have no neck.

I said no, and then he continued, grinning at the trap he'd set. "If you did, you'd never let that dog on that table."

I paused, thrown by this odd interaction. What did having children have to do with anything?

"So get the dog *off* the table," he said with a glint in his eye. I lured Toby down with a cookie, interrupting his glory, while Officer Marv nattered on about how the park was also for children and how dirty a dog was. I withheld eye contact from him and decided not to ask if he also hounded the squirrels who scampered over the sap-encrusted and dirt-caked picnic tables, or the parents who let their children eat off of them. When he was done, Toby and I walked on, with me feeling like a poisoner of children everywhere.

Of the forces bent on quashing the freedoms of the park, he was among the most malevolent. The only positive was the sense of unity that parkgoers felt in response to his sad power trip. There was a decent Animal Control officer who toured the parks in his little truck, issuing tickets and questioning miscreants. And in the summer, there were young rangers in training, who were chatty as they learned to exert themselves. They were all a breeze of sanity compared to Officer Marv, with his buzz cut and his razor tongue. To Officer Marv, dog owners weren't much different from thieves, and they were easier to corner and berate. He was in charge, and he loved to remind himself of that whenever he could.

If there was any doubt about Officer Marv's motives—you could argue he was protecting dogs and dog owners by keeping them in line, so the town wouldn't banish them from the parks—it was resolved one night, the Night of the White Dog. Push came to shove, and Officer Marv was no dove.

I was walking on the Amory Street border of the park with Nash and Hayley, and we saw a tall, white, fluffy mixed breed slowly emerge from the trees, off-leash and alone. His snout was long and his eyes were distant. It was a very cold early-March evening, and it had just gotten dark. He stood across the empty street from us, a ghostly lone-wolf vision with muddy feet and no collar. As we approached him and said, "Hey, buddy," he stepped away, wary. Nash stayed back with our dogs, all of them on their leashes. For each step Hayley and I carefully took toward the dog, he took two or three steps back. We stopped, took out cookies, and tried to lure him toward us. "Hey, buddy," we said again. We were still for a moment. And in an instant, he was gone, having slipped back into the darkness of the park. There was only a sliver of a silver moon low in the sky.

Hayley and I followed him into the trees, walking slowly, but we couldn't see any trace of his white figure. Right at that moment, Officer Marv pulled up and directed his cop car's bright white searchlight from the street into the park. Suddenly, the tree trunks and branches were artificially illuminated, as if we were on a movie set. He was on night duty. He yelled out to us, "What are you doing in there?"

We walked to his cruiser—it would take more than a few suspicious wanderers to get him to exert enough energy to get up from his driver's seat—and explained that we'd seen a lost dog in the park. We asked if he would shine that light deeper into the trees while we looked.

"Not my job," he said, "it's Animal Control's. I'll call them." Every second we waited, the white dog was wandering farther off; we imagined him veering into God knows what. Cars, fearful pedestrians, getting trapped in an abandoned basement, freezing cold—the possibilities were endless. When you imagine your own dog unattended in the world, afraid, it's unbearable. So Hayley, fired up, asked again, "Please, Marv, just a minute of light."

"Not my job," he responded again, holding on to his car microphone.

"What," she said, "it's not your job to be a human being?" It should have been a match on gasoline.

But the gasoline was really just a pot of beans, and Officer Marv ignored her, turned off his light, and drove off. Going after dogs, he must have felt, was not as much fun as going after people. We went and got Hayley's car, then turned the headlights on and aimed them into the park, but it was too little too late. The poor guy was gone or still lurking in the park, not responding.

The next morning, of course, there was no sign of the white dog at the park, and no talk of him, either. He'd slipped into the void that looms for all dogs off the leash—prowling alone in the night, not sure where to go, not recalling a home, defensive and hungry. A roving creature in a land of garbage cans and broken fences, looking off into the distance for something familiar. I shook my head again and hoped he'd found a warm couch, in spite of Officer Marv, and was sleeping on a full stomach at that exact moment, with a collar on.

That morning, when I saw Stan and Chewy at the park, I realized that the lost white dog had been a larger, more muscular version of Chewy. They were similar types; both had scruffy white faces and white golden retriever–like bodies. But the white dog had appeared to have a degree of cool, while Chewy was on edge, with her low-hind-leg posture and her knee-jerk fear. I thought of Chewy as being on the far side of the same journey that the white dog, if still unrecovered by caring owners, might just be starting. The white dog might be headed into the system, once someone managed to get hold of him, where his aloofness might erode into the kind of anxiety that now defined Chewy.

Chewy still couldn't bear eye contact with anyone except Stan, and even then it was quick. He'd get a blink from her. Otherwise, she'd hide directly behind a stranger like me at the park, rather than glance at his or her eyes. She was lovely—in the middle of her gorgeous vanilla coat, a smile with black lips—and people wanted to pet her. She was hard to miss as she scampered erratically amid the owners and the dogs like a pinball ball, and cookies were often proffered. But she just couldn't take one, no matter how much her stomach said yes.

The morning after the Night of the White Dog, I told Stan that it was my new goal to get Chewy to trust me, to take a cookie from my fingers, to look me in the face and share easy eye contact. It would be my personal challenge whenever I saw her. Stan enjoyed that idea. She should feel relief now, visiting the park every day to hang out, I thought. She should be able to play.

spring

the r. crumb cigar

To whom it may concern: Please excuse Matthew from sports to-
day, as he is not feeling quite well and he needs to recuperate. He
will be back in the swing of things soon!

As a profoundly unathletic kid, I forged school gym notes
as often as possible. I'd handwrite them with the flirty flour-
ishes I thought an attractive single mother might use, including, on one or two occasions, circle-dotted *i*'s and exclamation
points. I may have even floated a heart shape above some of
those *i*'s. Oddly, it worked every time, with help from thick
"adult" stationery and stiff envelopes. Sometimes, my decep-
tion successful, I'd smoke pot in a bathroom stall and go to
study hall to write something incomprehensible and purple for
my journal. I was a sports loser.

So it was with some disappointment and discomfort that,
as the winter snow and ice began to fade away, and as Toby's
fetching identity began to emerge fully, I realized I'd need
to deal with balls at the park for Toby. I saw what other retriever owners were obligated to do. I'd have to bring tennis
balls and squeaky balls every day, and keep track of the balls

if I didn't want to lose them. I'd have to throw the toys and the balls, maybe use a Chuckit to fling balls over other people's heads. I'd have to engage in endless ball fetching, pick up balls slimy with Toby's spit, and store balls in my car ad infinitum.

I couldn't ignore the fact that Toby was beginning to chase and catch round things and bring them almost back to me. Despite my ignorance of sports, and Tom's, too, Toby was a little jock. His retrieving nature was slowly elevating balls to the top of his list, just after food, with the biting of fingers and sleeves now becoming less urgent. He'd run full speed ahead, exuberant but serious, with his soft puppy eyes looking back at me as if he didn't quite know what he was running for, then realize, Oh, a ball. He'd pounce on it, head and front paws first, and grab it with great purpose, but then sniff something in the grass on his way back to me and drop it as if it were a meaningless object. He was lost in living.

Seeing Toby smile—and he did smile—as he waited for my arm to spring forth was a great incentive to deal with my ball issues. His silky ears would bounce and dance as he ran, and I would have all kinds of crazy love pangs.

"I am waiting, waiting, waiting," he'd say. "Still waiting."

And the thought that he wanted to bring something back to me and only me, that our connection was somehow written into his DNA, was touching. We were buds.

There at Amory to highlight my inadequacy was this guy, really a guy's guy, named Drew, who was at the park on weekend mornings.

"Hi, I'm Drew," he finally said after we'd seen each other a few times. We shook hands. He and his older dog, Chester, a still-strapping ridgeback mix, were an exceptional-looking pair as they gracefully played fetch. Drew had an ease about his carriage as he threw a yellow ball, standing apart from the group of people and dogs, watching the stately Chester canter and retrieve, canter and retrieve. Drew was a muscle-bound, low-key guy in jeans and sometimes a Springsteen T-shirt, not a snob, but not looking for big social activity, either. He had a dark, quiet brow, and his hair was always wet from the gym.

He was the guy who had put on oven mitts and delivered a pizza to Lucinda's front door a few years earlier, after her daughter had died, offering that touching combination of gentle sincerity and frozen food. Drew was someone who, without a dog at the dog park, I probably would have thought I'd have nothing in common with. But it turned out we had plenty to talk about, as he'd talk about his love life and I'd try to give him advice.

And Chester was a pumped guy, too, a lithe, short-coated brown dog whose ribs were detectable as he used every muscle at once to pursue the ball. He stayed around the fringes of the center of park activity with his owner, running and holding his yellow prize up in his bite for Drew to see. They were a caravan of physical twins and personality twins, too, content to play the same game with the same moves over and over. They formed a self-contained unit, loyal and a little aloof. They had a well-worn system, like a devoted married couple, but then Drew also liked to talk if you approached. Chester might ignore you, keep you out of his focus, but Drew fell into conversation.

I'd watch them carefully out of the corner of my eye. They made the whole ball thing look like an effortless, intimate partnership—a volley with a rigorous but not rigid flow. Chester would set off running for the ball before Drew threw it, trusting that Drew would land the ball where he was heading. Once the ball hit the ground in front of Chester, he snatched it in his mouth and did a slower, rounded, victory lap–paced turn back to Drew. Then he'd drop the ball right in front of Drew, a slimy yellow gift, and tear away for the next throw. There was something powerful about watching two beings know each other so well, so that each could give the other exactly what he wanted over and over again. If that's not closeness, then what is? Back and forth, back and forth. I knew Toby was ready to try that complete, circular understanding, but I wasn't. I felt like a bad doggy parent, holding my boy back from progress.

I'd rarely had to throw over the decades, but when the occasion did arise—I couldn't have skipped sports every day, could I?—I looked like a Tin Man windup toy. So I'd show up at Amory excruciatingly self-conscious and reticent about throwing for Toby, knowing that those people who were watching to see the cute puppy retrieve would see my struggle. I was a kid again. Like a cheap toy springing forward with a stuttering, mechanical jerk, I'd send the ball bouncing erratically a few feet in front of me. Each fling felt like some kind of public test or challenge, and there was an absurd amount of self-esteem at stake. Sometimes I'd resort to an underhanded throw, an open admission of deficiency.

Nash relished my throwing problem, as did Hayley. The gay guy who threw like a little girl—it was fodder for both of them.

"It's too easy," Nash would say.

There were a million gay stereotypes that did not fit me; the style gurus of cable TV would flunk me for my shabby T-shirts and forbid me to contact or go within one hundred yards of the word *fabulous*. But an athletic failure who'd always been picked last for team sports, who might have tripped on his way to kick a soccer ball, who had jumped aside when he was forced to play a guard during school football season—that dated chestnut fit me like a nonbaseball glove.

"It's too easy," Nash would say again.

They pitched the jokes at me—called me "Big Bird"—and I caught them. It was a game I enjoyed playing a lot more than this fetching business. Hayley loved to ask me about last night's basketball game, just to hear me say, "Wow, it was amazing. The way those guys hit that puck into the goal was awesome."

One March day, though, Nash instructed me as to the best positioning for throwing, so I wouldn't look stupid. It was an act of charity.

"Throw it to your side," he said, since I was pushing it straight in front of me like a geek. He took the tennis ball from me, showed me how to throw it, and I watched his arm cross in front of his face.

"It's like you're squeegeeing your face with your elbow?"

"Right," he said, "if that's how you need to see it."

Funny, how parental roles are not limited to parents, how friends and colleagues and spouses can become the father you didn't have, or the mother you did have. Dogs seemed to do that effortlessly, finding a family formation in every pack they stumbled upon. When she wasn't his older sister, Bertha was Toby's mother, or the Lucy to his Charlie Brown.

Nash threw the ball correctly a few times—over to the

side—albeit with some exaggeration, so I could see exactly what he was talking about. And I finally did it, and it worked. It gave me a not-so-ridiculous stance. Underneath the teasing, there was this support. It was an "aww" moment right out of a sitcom.

Balls. WTF? They are a central metaphor for masculinity, for nerve, for confusion, for the Earth—"this green ball which floats [us] through the heavens," which Emerson wrote in his essay "Nature." Balls are one of the most fundamental elements of play; they speak directly to that urge to be amused. There's an electricity about them, a reactive energy, as we try to control the randomness of their bounce and roll.

They are the focus of parks around the world, from the mass ball worship at Fenway Park in Boston, a few blocks from Amory, to the primary-colored children's balloons that float like giant sour balls above the grass on hot summer days—Georges Seurat in Technicolor. Like so many things in the dog park, from the charging dogs to the anonymity of their owners, balls brought people back to almost primitive feelings. They made me think of the genius of Charles Schulz, whose *Peanuts* turned a simple football, the round-headed Charlie Brown, dust, and the exclamation "AAUGH!!" into a prehistoric backyard play about life and love. It was a perfect flourish when Tom Hanks, alone and reduced to a state of basic need, fell in love with a Wilson volleyball in the movie *Cast Away*.

One day in early spring, still learning the art of the throw, I sprung a ball for Toby and it went a little bonkers. It bounced like mad, with no pattern, and landed close to a lady with a shih tzu. I'd seen her before, and she was overprotective of her dog—even though he was a fierce alpha who could scare the scruff up on a much bigger dog—and she was guarded around other people.

When she saw the ball, before Toby reached it, she turned quickly to me and said, "Did you throw that at me?" It was one-third question, two-thirds accusation. She flared up, and it was so out of character with the day and the mild March weather and the location, with its weeping willows and gentle hill. She looked classically ugly at that moment, scowling, except that she was really an attractive woman in her forties with curly hair. She was having a bad day, or a bad life, or she just didn't like the sight of me—I'd felt that kind of immediate antipathy before, sometimes at the park. I laughed nervously and Toby and I veered away. Just one of those irritations unworthy of brain storage, a reminder of where I didn't want to be.

Did I throw the ball at her? The question really was, Could I ever in a million years direct something specifically at anyone or anything in particular? Nope. It landed near her completely randomly, but for her that simple rubber sphere, like a small cannonball, had ignited a momentary firestorm. Balls. WTF?

Around that time, Toby was in love with a yellow rubber miniature football, which other dogs always wanted to steal from him.

He'd clench it in his teeth, and it looked like a protruding cigar as drawn by artist and comics illustrator R. Crumb—a fat yellow cartoon stogie with nibs on it. He'd gotten the football from Hayley, who'd gotten it as a gift for Stewie, who didn't like it, so Hayley had presented it to Toby. And Toby fell hard. He thought Hayley's yellow football was the giant key to confidence and power. It was a third as big as his head. He held it tilted up in his bite, despite its weight, for minutes at a time, Toby's visual statement of pride, a cigar that definitely wasn't a cigar. He was so in love with it that when we'd pull into the park, it seemed as though he was looking at me with extra eye-darting excitement, waiting for me to pull it out of the toy bag I kept in the passenger well of the car.

The R. Crumb cigar was legendary for him. People began to laugh along with him as he trotted by with extra bounce, this Flinstonian object protruding from his face.

One day after an unexpected March snow, Toby let go of it for a minute to go find his spot and poop, and while I was watching him, grabbing a bag from my pocket and preparing my poop mime, I noticed that Travis, with Margo nowhere in sight, was now running around with the football, bright yellow glaring out from his mouth like a lemon peel.

I called out to him, "Travis, come here, boy," but no luck. He ignored me, just as he ignored Margo, his long reddish ears shimmying as he pranced, savoring his new prize. I tried to seduce him with a cookie but only managed to entice Toby. When a dog won't drop a toy for a dog biscuit, you know you're in trouble.

Minutes passed. Toby stood watching as I struggled to recover his prize from Travis; occasionally, he ran toward Travis tentatively, then returned to me. It's strange trying to take control of someone else's dog, no matter how well you know that dog. I felt as if I were in Margo's house, among her things, alone.

Eventually, I gave up and found Margo ensconced in a conversation with Nash about finding peace in the modern world, maybe, or something biggish. They were locked in eye contact, Travis the furthest thing possible from Margo's mind. Bertha sat panting lazily at their feet, while in the background, Toby continued to make tentative moves toward Travis, romping behind him like a zigzagging kite. I stood close by Margo and Nash and slipped into their conversation, then mentioned the fact that Travis had gone off with Toby's toy. I said, "You know, his beloved favorite-ever yellow rubber R. Crumb cigar football thingy from Hayley that everyone loves seeing."

"Look at that guy," I said pointing to Travis. "He has fallen in love."

Margo distractedly looked in her bag, pulled out a tennis ball, and handed it to me. "Will he like this?" she said with a smile, nodding at Toby. That was it, and she turned back to her conversation about the soul and the mind and whatnot. I stood holding the dry, dirty, generic green ball and watched while Toby now stood in place, looking longingly at Travis as he showed off the yellow football, the older brother flaunting his superiority.

I'm not gonna lie. I was a little miffed. The trade was definitely not fair. I didn't want to be petty; I'd seen dog owners who monitored their dog's toys too fiercely, who showed up with fabulous squeaky balls, then pouted and argued and got irrational when other dogs inevitably went after them.

"Dutchess would sure like Kona to give her back her ball now" was how that particular ventriloquism would start.

It didn't take long to learn that many dogs at the park liked toys and balls, but they yearned for and loved another dog's toy or ball with special intensity. The other dog's grass was always greener, too. But still, it looked as though Travis was going to chew up Toby's adored toy right in front of him, while Margo, earth mother, my new friend, remained lost in her cosmic chat with Nash. Travis settled down with the yellow football and began to gnaw at it conspicuously with his front teeth.

I called Toby and we left without the toy, Toby running ahead happily, Margo's old tennis ball in his mouth, and me, irritated, not moving on.

Strangely enough, a day or two later the thin layer of snow started melting and the rubbery R. Crumb cigar emerged. It was shiny, half-buried in the slush, cold, and clean, as if brand-new. There were bite marks on it, but they'd been scrubbed free of their dirt by the icy water. Travis must have dropped it. Toby quickly spotted the happy yellow and hopped over to it, his wagging tail shaking his whole bottom half as he picked it up in his mouth and held it high. A triumph! He brought it over and danced in front of me in classic Snoopy fashion. The R. Crumb cigar!

And then I saw Hayley in boots and a ponytail trudging toward us through the slush with Stewie in tow and her hand in her pocket, pulling out another R. Crumb cigar and holding it out toward us. She'd felt bad that Toby had lost his football to Travis—I'd complained to her—so she'd gone out and bought him a new one. I laughed at the coincidence as she gave it to me, a bright heart of gold.

It was visually weird to see two identical yellow footballs in one place, brilliant against the rampant gray of the slushy day, and it was comforting, too. There was a karmic system of some kind at play, when it came to toys and other good things. The park, at best, could be a lovely chain of gift giving, in-kind exchanges, and petty theft. There was an emotional ecosystem, whereby most people wound up somewhere toward the middle of the "giveth" and the "taketh away" ends of the spectrum. The same thing happened with umbrellas on the party circuit. Would Margo bring me a yellow football, too? Leaving Toby and me with three R. Crumb treasures? No, that didn't happen. But some other day, I was sure, she would drop some good toy for Toby and, on her way out of the park ask, "Will he like that?" With her casual manner, she would inadvertently remind me that lost things do return, if in a different form. The dogs run in great circles, and so do we.

Eventually, Toby and I headed back to the car and left Amory that day, two happy dogs with two fat yellow footballs.

cell phone lady

The more I talked to Hayley, the more I liked her. You could get into little romantic friendships with people as you stood together for hours every week. I knew that kind of rapport wasn't unique to the dog park, but it was easier to find there, in that informal microcosm, than out in the world. The dogs, with their crashes and chases and their contagious contentedness, made it happen. Hayley and I understood early on that we were on the same wavelength, and when we weren't, we were able to point that out to each other.

"Are you're saying I am too sensitive?" she asked me when we were talking about why she disliked a guy with a Yorkie, a man she thought had snubbed her.

"No, I'm saying everyone else isn't sensitive enough."

One day at Amory in early March, I was on the phone with my brother in Philadelphia, standing on the outskirts of the group of people and dogs as Toby zoomed here and there with his R. Crumb cigar. My brother David and I talked every day, gossiping about family and setting sick and twisted jokes to the tune of Hebrew prayers, or Joni Mitchell songs, or radio hits from our childhood. It was demented, our weird language together. Hayley came up beside me and stood waiting for me to get off, which I did quickly, feeling awkward.

"I like to leave my phone at home," she volunteered.

Her thick hair tucked back behind her ears, she was smirking about her own boldness in confronting me. She said she treated the park as a call-free zone, a break from the beast. How sad, she said, to be miles away while your dog was playing joyously at your feet. Didn't Toby deserve better?

It smacked of the kind of thinking that demonized all the great new technology we live with. My brother and I had remained in sync with each other across the years, despite the distance, largely thanks to our cell phones and to e-mail. That was a great thing, right?

But I was persuaded, too, as we talked it through. The idea of a daily intermission from the virtual, a spot of sun through the cloud, appealed. Like the rest of civilization, I was leashed to my devices, as well as to my Facebook friends and my twenty-four-hour news scroll. It was the last frontier in self-protection and emotional distance, to be somewhere and yet still psychically somewhere else. These devices were very high-tech tools with which to make a very primitive kind of flight. You were in a room or on a street or at a park, and a very beautiful park at that, but only partially there—I knew that state intimately, long before cell phones arrived.

With my *Globe* job, I always had the sense that my life was super full as I skipped from my TV screen to my computer screen to my phone and back, looking and checking; but then, looming, there was "the barrenness of a busy life," as Socrates put it. It was time to check myself. Actually, I began to fall in love with the idea of a daily "off," and wished some younger generation would embrace it, turn it into a rebellion in an unexpected swing of the pendulum.

Toby's name closely resembles "to be"—that had been my idea when Tom and I named him, thinking of a *Globe* editor who'd killed himself shortly before we got Toby; that friend, so overwhelmed and resigned, had chosen not to be. Time to be, I thought, at least for a few hours a day. So I took Hayley's advice that day and tried to stay in the moment of the park, at the park.

And there was Saul, doing his circles, reminiscing with strangers about his youth while forgetting yesterday, smiling at all passersby, a reminder of how "to be" is only a step ahead of "was."

Back in December, watching two dogs play together with Margo had been like dancing together. It was very "to be." That day early on, with Toby and Travis wrestling at our feet, was the first time I'd been conscious of finding dog play so deeply pleasurable and diverting. Dog play cut through all the ambiguous human signals out there in our collective awareness, and through all my personal restraints. It landed us in the present tense. Toby and Travis were actually moving Margo and me that day, compelling us to be happy and unself-conscious. Yes, dogs can be our dummies, our verbal and psychological outlets, but Margo and I were their puppets, stomping and bending toward them with belly-deep laughs. There were a number of those great play days.

And another day, sunny despite the clouds, Margo and I

had the occasion to dance together again, unexpectedly, this time not over dogs. Again, we found ourselves thinking about nothing outside of the dog park, reveling in a state of "to be."

It was early April, we were walking through the middle of Amory, and it seemed like no one else was there. By now, Toby and Travis were playing on their own around us, two yellowish red creatures jumping and chasing, Travis still the boss. And then suddenly, a tall woman named Claude, whom I'd seen a few times, appeared with her dog Panda, her shoulder bag filled with squeaky toys and fat novels and cigarettes. Panda, a gray midsize mutt, walked proudly behind her and then sneaked ahead to sniff Toby and Travis. We stopped and talked, and it was clear we all felt good that day, a small pleasure day, as Toby, Travis, and Panda jockeyed around us. We were jokey and caffeinated. Claude, holding a giant take-out coffee, was definitely in the mood to talk.

Wearing a blazer streaked from painting houses, Claude put her coffee down on the ground, lit up a cigarette, then picked up her coffee. She had a lot to say about the beautiful day, the muscular clouds, the arrival of spring, and how the bare tree branches would soon be closely lined with green and red buds. Eventually, somehow, Shakespeare came up. Did Claude bring him up? Or was it one of us? I can't recall. But she stood talking about Shakespeare, this towering woman, and asked if we wanted to hear her do some Shakespeare. Yes. And which Shakespeare should she do? We said off the top of our heads, "*Macbeth*."

Then, as if it were no big trick, she started delivering passages from *Macbeth*, seriously long passages. And she recited both sides of the dialogue, the words spoken with a great tragic passion that was infectious. Claude was fully being a character, making each phrase mean something, and then she was on the other side, facing a different sun and being someone else, all expressive brows and nose. The cigarette was stomped out, the coffee on the ground.

It was mesmerizing. Claude went on effortlessly for five or ten minutes, impromptu, a sustained jig on her own in the park.

That which hath made them drunk hath made me bold;
What hath quench'd them hath given me fire. Hark! Peace!

She was really sending out those lines. She got lost in it, like someone from another age, the tall, grimy Elizabethan street performer. It was all off the top of her head, flowing. Meanwhile, Toby and Travis played around us and Panda sat panting. How much could this woman have memorized, that she could just go on like that? Her lines seemed freshly rehearsed, but she couldn't have prepared them, because she would have had no idea which play we'd choose. Clearly, she took the poetry seriously, and she probably recited it to herself all day long on ladders while painting.

Will all great Neptune's ocean wash this blood
Clean from my hand? No, this my hand will rather
The multitudinous seas incarnadine,
Making the green one red.

We were under her spell. Somewhere in the middle of the Shakespeare, drifting in Claude's flow, Margo and I had nudged the arms of each other's jackets, blown away by this vision of dirty longhaired actors in capes, jousting in the forest. It was some nameless afternoon in the park, but here was this little eternity, with Margo next to me, dancing in her clogs, riveted.

"Had enough?" Claude asked once or twice, breaking out of her show and looking at us. We replied, "No way."

When Claude eventually rounded up Panda and moved on after another five minutes, not quite aware of her impact, Margo and I were left a bit dazed, as if a dream had just come to a close. We'd been transported. It was crazy. Shakespeare in the park. Claude was another one of the people I would probably never have met except at the dog park, outside my loop of home, TV, the *Globe,* and loved ones. She wasn't among my list of Facebook friends. She was a surprise out of the blue on that bright day.

I looked Margo in the face and said, "That was crazy," a vague question mark lingering at the end of the sentence. It had been so bizarre.

She looked straight at me, her rectangles smiling, shaking her head in disbelief. And then she said, laughing, as if we'd just shared exactly the same hallucination, "No, that was craaaazy."

Claude was in the moment, and she made a moment for Margo and me. Cell Phone Lady was not in the moment. They made a perfect contrast, it seemed. That April, a stout woman with a brown shag haircut started coming to Amory, climbing out of her low beige sedan with a cell phone forever cradled between her shoulder and her ear.

Talking, she would let her two Westies out of the backseat, then follow the pair of white pom-poms off the tar and around the grass, never looking up, idly holding empty poop bags in one hand like little jib sails. It was painful to watch her twisting her neck out of alignment to keep the phone in place, looking and nodding into the middle distance as she talked at length, a yoga stretch held eons too long. Now in her forties, she was heading toward some very expensive later-life chiropractic sessions.

Hayley and I hated her right away. Whenever she'd pull into the parking lot, we'd look at each other and raise our eyebrows. "Hate her." Here she comes, the lady who doesn't care about being here, twilight-zoning her way through this beautiful place with a big magnet stuck to her ear. We had attitude about it. For a half hour, she'd linger on the phone, ambling, her dogs drifting together by themselves ahead of her on the field, an absentminded shepherd with her flock of two. Sometimes you could hear her voice, though not her words, drifting on the breeze. Her dogs didn't interact with the other dogs at the park, and as if they sensed the Cell Phone Lady's bubble of untouchability, the other dogs barely noticed the Westies. Even Saul didn't bother trying to break into her closed-off environment, and I wondered if he was probably brooding over her, too, along with the *Bride of Frankenstein* lady.

Finally, she'd click the phone off as she returned to the parking lot, and they'd all get back in her car. It was as though the park was merely a necessity in her day, to be gotten through, like taking out the garbage. She wasn't a high-fashion type, with her walking sneakers and mom jeans, but she was on another plane as she and her dogs stepped around the outskirts of the groupings of people in her path. If she'd been aware of her surroundings, she might have felt us sending negative vibes her way, but she was too far gone.

Cell Phone Lady looked a bit like her dogs—feathered hair, wandering forward close to the ground. She seemed weighted down by the world. Her conversations didn't appear to be particularly cheerful ones, her mouth straight and her footsteps arrhythmic and heavy. In triangular formation, she and the dogs seemed to be operating on a level of subconsciousness together as they wound slowly away from others, another little caravan of issues. She was the absentee leader, walking behind them, in another world, out of touch. At least the dogs have each other, I thought.

One day, she showed up, and midway into her shoulder-led trip through the park, she clicked off her phone and put it in her pocket. Her call had ended.

Her bubble popped, she stood blinking, looking up. It was strange, and she seemed lost, standing there on the field without her crutch. Her dogs, sniffing the ground side by side, didn't notice. It might have been the first time she'd really looked at the place, taken in the reality of the trees and the grassy hill and the other owners.

I saw my chance, split off from the group of people and dogs, and moved toward her, Toby skipping at my side. I was feeling nosy and forward, a little bit like an investigator, or maybe like a dog park wack job.

"Hello, Cell Phone Lady," I said as I approached. She laughed—either because she knew why I'd called her that or because it was her default off-guard expression. It was a hearty laugh, and she clearly took no offense. Suddenly, I was very curious about who she was.

She brought an unexpected amount of eye contact to our encounter, and she said, "Hello, park person." Again, she laughed.

It was day and night, my impression of her, the way it switched over in a moment like a page in a book. Suddenly, I wanted to be on her side. Toby headed over toward the Westies, sniffing and sniffing. It was as if he'd sensed my shift in reaction.

"What are your dogs' names?" I asked. She was with "Miss Midge and Miss Hope, three and eight," she said, and they were all on a break from work. She said something about how they loved getting away from "the house," and then later she said something about "the clients," so I asked where she worked. She was the manager of a halfway home for intellectually challenged youths a few blocks away, and she was on her lunch break but still in contact with the other counselors at the house as to how the clients were doing.

This was her time to coach and supervise. Sometimes the counselors needed pep talks; burnout was common in her field, she said. She found she could muster good advice and positive energy when she was away from everything for a few minutes. The clients at the house loved the dogs, too, and she was glad about that. Midge and Hope were a healing presence, with Midge the grande dame of the whole human-dog litter. The kids really lit up when the dogs were underfoot. And she lit up when she told me that, her puffy eyes taking on a little sparkle. She had a little bit of dam burstage as she went on about all the special times the clients would have playing with

Midge and Hope, and how dogs had always been her savior when she was young and afraid.

In short, Cell Phone Lady was the best person ever, a combat fighter in the war for the needy and helpless. She was completely sympathetic, and her love of the park was real, if entirely different from mine. It gave her freedom from her routine, a little slack on her leash. Like me, she let go at Amory; we were just letting go of very different things.

I'd gotten her caravan entirely wrong. She was the backbone of their trio, just getting a stretch. She was so damned maternal and giving, there for all those kids and colleagues and dogs. I felt like a silly fool for having judged her, and so did Hayley when I told her.

"You mean WE were wrong?" she asked, a flash of irony in her voice.

From that point on, when we saw Cell Phone Lady on the field, doing her thing, straining and straining her neck, we nodded at each other. "Love her."

sparks

Every time I noticed the Cell Phone Lady at Amory from that point on, I'd wave to her, and she'd wave back with a free hand. I didn't know her name, but that didn't matter—it rarely does at the park. I knew she was with Midge and Hope, and that was enough. It felt like a small victory and a relief to let go of my judgment of her. But there was something I couldn't easily let go of that spring.

As I've mentioned, people talked about poop a lot at the park, despite the fact that it's not considered polite conversation. But they rarely talked about humping. As a brand-new freshman in the quad, Toby would occasionally get humped by the senior dogs. Two or three older park snouts would take in Toby's scent and push down possessively in between his shoulders. And then a dog would climb up onto his back, even a smaller dog, rhythmically moving his or her hips against Toby's blond back as if Barry White music were playing over giant speakers.

It didn't matter if a male or a female was doing the mounting, since most of the park dogs, like Toby, had been neutered;

they just stood grasping Toby's back, basking in a bit of dominance, and in the case of Toby, safe dominance. He was no threat, which suited the more insecure seekers.

As they humped him, Toby's blasé gaze said, "I can chase that ball when you're done."

Other humpees might vehemently resist getting humped, giving a toothy warning snarl at the humper and a quick body shift, but not my passive little goose. He treated the events like short intermissions in the play action.

I noticed how they always looked so proud, the humpers, showing all the world they were the boss. That was the point of the hump—that public statement of superiority, the serious look on the face of this sheltie or that golden retriever, like one of *Playboy*'s old suave, self-satisfied men in a silk bathrobe. While riding his or her conquest, the humper wore a wooden, primitive mask–like expression of contentment and power, not male or female so much as just unspecific supremacy.

Park humping was a reminder of the profound nakedness of dog behavior, which isn't mitigated by layers of clothing or by language. People stand around in civilized interaction, frictionless, with their rules of proximity and their fleece, while dogs simply knock into each other. They're our friends, and we've bred them over the centuries to be like us, and they are like us in many, many ways; but yeah, they're also animals who can lick their own butts, and do.

There were other vaguely sex-related dog moments at the park, aside from humping, such as when you needed to sneak a glimpse at a dog's genitals to know if said dog was a he or a she.

"Breaking news," Margo said one day, returning to the

group after retrieving Travis after he'd taken a Border collie named Polly's ball. We'd generally seen Polly only from afar as she circled the park with her owner, both distant. "Paulie," she said, after getting a good look, "is a boy."

But it was another thing to watch a sex act being simulated while standing with a bunch of dog owners, including old ladies with Chihuahuas and teenagers and parents with infants in Snuggies. You felt as if you'd all been transported to the set of a porn movie.

A lot of the dog activity at the park was disinhibiting, liberating for the more resistant among us who needed to be pushed into play and pleasure. The dog wrestling and the fighting and barking sparked spontaneity in the owners. It was a place to be loose. But humping evoked an X-rated vibe that pushed the boundaries of mixed company. It made many of us clench with embarrassment as we projected our human cultural taboos onto our pets.

By the way, we did have a human sexual story line lurking in the backdrop at the park, one that Hayley pointed out to me. A man and a woman, both in their forties, met every weekday at Amory at about 4:00 P.M.

"Watch this," Hayley would say.

In the parking lot, the woman would arrive in a Honda Civic, park next to the guy's red truck, and climb into the passenger seat. After a kiss and a few minutes of talking, the pair would set out into the small woods behind the parking lot, a nature preserve with a pond and a few geese, an area that wasn't open to dogs. A half hour later, they'd return and sit in the truck, talking. We were sure they were having an affair; why else meet at the park? Some days, one would show and not the other.

They'd say hello to the park regulars, thinking we were in on their secret, or entirely unaware that we were in on their secret. The guy occasionally struck up small talk with Hayley about the weather or about the Red Sox when they passed each other in the parking lot. "Hey," he'd say.

And I once saw Saul engaging them, telling them stories, as they stood outside of the truck, leaning, nodding at him.

I saw that some humper owners were copacetic about the humping phenomenon. They'd say things to me like "That's just what they do; that's natural," wait to see if I really minded if Toby got humped, and then let it be or interrupt it accordingly. And others were instantly horrified and grabbed their dog by the collar and said "NO," trying to interrupt the basic urge in their dogs. They were disgusted at the sight, no matter how I felt about it. Humping . . . bad.

I was uncomfortable with the publicness of humping, I have to admit, and I wanted it to end—even while I understood that it was just communication between animals. If a dog was on Toby, doing the humpty duty, moving his hips in a rubbery movement, I couldn't relax. It was silly, in a way, because it was just the dogs miming hierarchy, but I felt more unnerved with each new thrust. I wanted to be a person who could shrug his shoulders at animal behavior, but I couldn't turn off the projection of human attributes onto dogs; I'd been turning Toby more and more into my child with each passing week, and that made it difficult. He was the epitome of innocence to me, a little play-obsessed guy who belonged to us. I'd kiss his snout and know exactly where it had been. Letting him enter into his own social situation was a new thing.

One dog, Atlas, was a tall poodle mix with chocolate brown fur that shook like a 1980s Tina Turner wig when he ran. That spring, Atlas just had to hump Toby no matter what. I'd see a shady look come over Atlas's eye the minute Toby arrived at the park, and then I'd see a shady look come over his owner Harry's eye, as if to ask if I minded. Toby was so new, his coat so bright, and I knew it wasn't sexual—but still, as the coarse, shiny fur on Atlas' hind legs undulated and Toby just stared ahead, I felt I wanted Atlas off him. At that time, it was too much. I'd politely ask Harry to stop the humping if he could, then watch him drag his sweet dog away. I'd feel bad about it. But still. My baby. It was irrational.

Naturally, there were attractions among the dog people, romantic comedies that played out quietly while the dogs were off the leash.

It wouldn't have been a special, disencumbering place if there weren't some love among the humans as they stood among the terriers and retrievers. All the fevered play, the dogs wrestling from bottom to top and back again, jawing one another's necks and nosing one another's bellies, it prodded the unconscious. The willows stood eternally restful on the eastern border of Amory field, spring arrived, the elegant herons passed over on their way to the neighboring pond, and paradise aroused longing.

I knew Hayley was lonely behind her flippancy and humor, and, as her final semester began to wind up, I knew she was wondering if Boston was wrong for her. She wasn't buttoned-down enough for this town, as she spoke her mind without careful editing. At the park, where people yelled and oddballs found a niche, where Noreen was a beloved icon, Hayley was another player in the band. But, at thirty, she was not making the expected segue into dinner-party circles, and at the same time she was getting too old for the Allston bar scene, where you either screamed over the music all night long or stood watching before going home alone.

She had a rich complexion, which would flush on cold days and, framed by her brown hair, make her look almost tan. At times, I romantically imagined her as a Victorian duchess with a passion for riding horses in the English countryside. I was touched by her solo charge into battle. But I could see that, secretly, she was longing just to find peace, and a partner.

It wasn't hard for me to figure out that she'd set her sights on Drew, and that she was going to be the aggressor. Like me, she'd admired how he played fetch with Chester, as he threw the ball so confidently and Chester returned it so loyally. Caravan Drew.

"Now that's some fetching fetching," she'd say.

Standing with me around 9:30 A.M. on weekends, she'd keep one eye on the parking lot for Drew until he arrived in his black SUV, and she made sure Chester knew to come nosing into her silver down jacket pocket for treats. She'd confessed her crush to me, and I'd suggested, cautiously, that she should save her energy. From what I could tell, Drew was a bit of a player and Hayley didn't stand a chance. But Hayley was not one to give up easily in any endeavor once she'd made up her mind.

Watching her work was touching. She was a knight wearing metal gloves, trying to knit a dainty little mitten. While Drew faithfully threw the yellow ball for Chester, his gym-body arm flexing his T-shirt sleeve tight, his pitch-black hair wet and slicked back, Hayley faced his way and talked as Stewie chased Toby and Toby chased Chester in a chain of cheerful fools. She knew Drew liked the Rolling Stones, and so she asked him questions about them.

"How does Mick keep his energy so high?"

More often, she'd say, "Chester is such a sweet dog. I love him!" The ventriloquism was obvious. You could feel her trying.

As Drew looked into the distance at Chester fetching and returning, he'd smirk at what she said, amused by her efforts, willing to make a few typical-guy comebacks to keep her interested. She was throwing the ball; he was just throwing it back.

we are saul

Old Saul was still driving. Watching him float slowly down into the parking lot in his white sedan became a daily bit of suspense. He'd creep along, a tin caterpillar, pulling into a space ever so carefully. Nash, Margo, and I would be on proverbial tenterhooks, hoping he wouldn't hit anything in his uncertain maneuvers.

"Pleeeease make it," Margo would say.

You could tell that his sense of space was off as he glided a little too closely to parked cars, a few scratches already marking his flanks. If there were dogs running nearby, we prepared to scream out if they headed too close to him. After parking, he'd sit for a moment at the wheel, collect himself, his gray head still, then get out and start walking along the park paths, trusty flip-up shades flipped up, looking out from the deck of a boat with the reflection of sun on ocean in his eyes.

He'd circle the park slowly and deliberately, and it was more like he was standing on an unanchored rowboat on a calm day, drifting forward, than on anything with engines and a ship's wheel. And he faced a little traffic, not just from the dog people but from joggers and bicyclists, and one speed walker in particular, his *Bride of Frankenstein* lady.

That spring, in what was a little sunrise-sunset pairing, a mother from the neighborhood would occasionally accompany her four- or five-year-old son in loops around the park as the kid practiced riding his bike with training wheels. Saul was slow, and the mother would make sure the boy, a blond and friendly little man, went far around the old man, out of respect and so as not to throw him off balance. She'd guide him around the dogs, too. As the kid biked ahead of Saul, Saul would smile and nod his gray head to the mother as she passed him on foot, and she would smile back. She got it.

The kid, in his shiny black helmet, trying to focus on the road like a race-car driver, was all alertness, while Saul was so obviously on the ebb.

You figured it out. The first time Saul asked you your dog's name and breed, it was a sweet encounter with an old guy. By the fifth time in a week, you understood that his memory was clouding, that he was drifting off course.

"She's still a dachshund," someone might say to him, trying to make a little joke.

He'd smile back; smiling was always his first response. When you engaged with him, he talked more and more about having been a musician, and you could picture him with a trombone, playing old-time music. Whether or not he actually ever performed was unclear. I'd listen to his slow sentences and picture him in the band at some kind of swing jazz club, the young, soft-spoken little-brother type, ever observant amid the band sounds and crazy nights.

And so it became known to everyone who came regularly to Amory that he was nearing the end of his conscious life, still just able to drive from home to the park and back, not much else. The dogs didn't bother with him; they sensed his distance. But he was content, it seemed, despite being disoriented, and he was gentle. A few of the dog people investigated and learned that he had no children, that he was living with a brother, and that that brother was aware Saul was on the wane. So Saul had backup, in addition to the dog park; that was good to know.

One day, Nash, Margo, and I saw Saul pull into a parking spot and begin his wandering, looking ahead at the small clusters of people and dogs around Amory, hoping to strike up conversation. Saul being Saul. We laughed together for a minute as we spotted him heading step by step toward some new prey across the park, preparing to ask the person, "What's your dog's name?" and "How old is he?" and "What is the breed?"

Those were the same questions we'd ask newcomers as we did our own circling of Amory, every day, all week. It was uncanny.

We looked at one another. "We are Saul," Nash said. "We ARE Saul." We kept laughing. Yup, there were funny, weird, sad similarities between Saul's life and our own. Sailing into the next phase, the park our anchor, we were all Saul.

A cloth sack of dog toys showed up on one of the picnic tables that same week. There were squeaky toys, balls of different colors and textures, tennis balls, and, saddest of all, a leash.

At first, as Margo and I approached the table, we thought someone had actually forgotten their stuff.

"What a hassle," she said. "Whoever it is will have to come all the way back to the park."

"I know. Hope no one steals anything," I said. A few of the items were already out of the bag, as if someone had been picking through the collection for the best toys. A hard blue ball with some kind of jingle inside sat calling out to me, since I knew Toby would love it. He and Travis were busy playing, Toby jumping at Travis as Travis held a tennis ball in his jaw, and I was tempted to introduce the blue ball into their dynamic.

And then, at exactly the same moment, Margo and I both realized what the bag meant. A dog had died, and the owner had wanted or needed to get the belongings out of the house. In an act of charity, he or she had left the precious goods at Amory. We looked at each other, I said, "Oops," and we went in for a hug. We patted each other's backs affectionately.

"Aww," she said, "that's just too grim."

It was. But thinking about aging and death hadn't been uncommon or even unpleasant for me during most of my life. I was drawn to it, as if I carried a hidden Geiger counter that could detect particles of loss.

On long solo walks around Boston before Toby, listening to bittersweet playlists on my iPod, I'd start imagining everyone who had ever meant anything to me on their deathbeds, my eyes locked on theirs, real in the face of finality, the home at the end of the world; I'd picture my father, at age thirty-seven, weak from bad blood, thinking of his children and wife as he let go and disappeared.

I'd get all sniffly and tragique as I walked along the broad Charles River or past the brownstone storefronts of Back Bay, a designated mourner moved by the tragedy of time. It felt good; it really did. I was morbid Harold in the 1970s cult film *Harold and Maude,* before the revelation of Maude.

The thought of getting a dog, once I'd warmed up to dogs, was checked by my tendency toward anticipatory grief. Why would anyone let themselves love a dog? I'd think. Why would anyone invest their tenderness and devotion and need in a creature that stays for only a dozen or so years—thirteen maybe, if you're lucky, fourteen if you're supremely blessed? In the course of an average human lifetime, pots and pans and couches and lamps stay with us for longer stretches of time. Even beloved T-shirts survive the decades, the silk-screened album images and tour dates wrinkled and cracked but still holding on. With a dog, you're on a fast train to heartache. Such were the ideas that ran through my broody brain.

So as I watched little Toby grow every day, counting his age in weeks and months, I would easily fall into a sweet melancholy state. It was funny, how I could bring almost anything around to death, including a puppy. In his ninth month, Toby was still all goofiness, still a little genius when it came to stealing shoes and luring Tom and me into a house chase. But his blond Lab forehead and cheeks were starting to lose their extra, furrowed skin as his chest dropped and his legs got lanky. His yellow body fur was still so soft and fine, a tactile revelation, like the feel of an ultrasoft brush on your cheek; but on his back, a line of coarse water-resistant hairs was starting to emerge. He was thickening, growing up and away already, it seemed, before he'd even hit one.

Tugging on Toby's ears, kissing his snout like a kiss-crazy fool while he tolerated my attentions, I'd have that feeling of unhindered love and mushiness coupled with doom, the sense of having gained something unimaginably sweet and losing it at the very same moment. "Don't it always seem to go," Joni Mitchell wrote, "that you don't know what you've got till it's gone"; I knew what I had gotten, because I anticipated him gone every single day. I'd look Toby straight in his root beer brown eyes and well up with love and loss, the two sentiments bound to each other like a cluster of molecules, then feel a little guilty about imagining his end right in front of his innocent, fuzzy baby face, before his life had truly begun.

That I was thinking about Toby leaving, even as he slimed my cheeks and mouthed at my hands and my hoodie strings, was a strange compliment. It meant that he'd touched me, that after a short time I already knew I'd miss him in a big way. He'd entered my very exclusive grief club; maybe he'd be on my Mount Rushmore of anticipated grief, next to Tom, and my brother, and my mother.

Toby didn't grieve, unless it was for the stuffed toy he'd just disemboweled in a fit of instinct or for the bowl of food he'd just inhaled. He'd always look at me for what would be next, hoping there would be more.

Standing with Margo at that table of toys, I understood that the park, with its rules and rituals and tennis balls and poop bags and face-offs and lovefests, had become my Maude. It was my place not to be watching TV with a remote control in my hand, not to be on my cell phone, not to be alone and grieving.

We all need a Maude.

as the table turns

And then one April day, and then another April day, Toby humped a dog.

Overnight, my little Mr. Peabody, my playful fellow with the long blond ears and happy dance, had turned into an occasional dominator. It was a rude awakening. Toby, our little boy, our best buddy, who determinedly came running and jumped onto the bed when Tom and I yelled "Family meeting," the little goose at our feet with the stuffed animals in his mouth, was thrusting in public. It's one of those awkward moments, when you are so acutely reminded of the fact that your buddy is an animal. There he was, atop another dog, looking ahead with that glaze over his eyes.

There I was on the other side. It happened rarely, but it happened. Now I was the guy with the shady eye. It was just little Toby playing at being a big shot, as I'd begun to understand it. Toby would hump another dog, and then eventually he would wind up underneath that dog, a game in which each got to be the king of the mountain. But I knew how the other owner might feel. I knew too well. And then, after pulling Toby away and leashing him, I might initiate a conversation about humping being about play and dominance and not necessarily sex.

And then I'd feel transgressive for talking about sex in such an everyday park environment with a complete stranger, especially if it was a lady with white hair and a metal cane and a little terrier named Buffy. And I'd officially become that person I once had observed with scorn, the one who talks to a stranger about sex and power without thinking twice, the weird park person with no boundaries in a pack of freaks.

I had to come to terms with Toby's sporadic need to hump. He'd been on the bottom—and still was when some dogs saw him—but now he wanted to be on top every now and then. I could see it in his eye when he detected a dog he could approach safely and hump. It was like gaydar, when you can sense a possible gay affiliation before anyone else. I sensed Toby's thinking— humpdar—the second he spotted new possibilities when they entered into the pack. I'd get this feeling in my gut; I could tell he was thinking about maybe seriously considering the possibility of jumping up on that dog to prove his status as the not-bottom of that particular grouping. And I would approach him to stop it before anything had happened. I'd lead him away, as Harry had ultimately led Atlas away.

Sometimes, it was easy. One Saturday, Toby set out on his mission to hump Chester. As Chester chased the yellow ball thown by Drew, who was dressed in his usual T-shirt, his hair wet, Toby chased Chester. It was great—both dogs were in motion, so Toby could make his move only when Chester was still, which was rare.

But I asked Drew if Toby's attentions were bothering him.

No, he said, that's fine. He laughed, and we proceeded to talk about dog behavior and music and I told him about humpdar, and he laughed some more.

We were amused by the innuendo of the conversation we were having on an ordinary weekend in the park. We liked each other, and as he told me more and more about his life as a young single guy, it was as I'd imagined—bars, texting, hook-ups, mornings after, sometimes mornings after that were that particular morning at the park. He felt trusting of me. He was trying to push away a local woman he'd been dating, who was calling and texting too often for his comfort; but then he was in hot pursuit of a woman he'd met during a trip to San Diego. Sometimes I wondered why he was sharing his torrid tales with me as my dog jogged after his dog. I decided that he saw me as a neutral, nonjudgmental party, one who could joke to his face about his commitment issues, which I did occasionally.

"The longer the plane ride, the better," I'd say.

Later, I told Hayley that I had developed humpdar, that I could see a humping event approaching, and she was amused, too. Hayley immediately asked the question foremost in her mind: If I was so good about predicting humping, could I see her and Drew getting together in the near future?

Other times, dog-humping events could turn ugly. That spring, a distinguished older guy started showing up with a young apricot cockapoo named Zelda. She had not been spayed, and one day, when she was coming out of her first heat, Toby was all over her. In the blink of an eye, my little guy was sniffing after her and making the moves. He'd been neutered and there was no pink—no "lipstick," as some park people called it—and still he was psychically aroused and all about her. At the sight of Toby pursuing Zelda, when Toby was about to make the hump, Zelda's owner came to me with an anxious look in his dark eyes, which sat like ball bearings underneath thick, hairy eyebrows.

"Take him away," he said curtly.

I got the message and pulled Toby away from Zelda and over to the broad side of the field, two full baseball diamonds away. But when he saw his chance, when my guard was down, Toby tore all the way across the expanse to his beloved of the moment, Zelda. My little rebel ignored my increasingly loud calls, running like a freed prisoner. When I got there, Zelda's owner, Nick, was pulling Toby by his collar, red with anger, choking him perhaps more than he needed to. Nick looked as if he was tightening all the muscles on his body, as if his own manhood had been challenged.

"Here he is," Nick said, as if my puppy were some kind of dirty criminal.

"Are you planning to have her spayed?" I asked as I got there. He gave no answer. There was contempt and hostility in his demeanor. He handed me Toby's collar, and I hooked up my dog to the leash and led him away, ultimately back to the car to leave. It was troubling, both to see Toby so persistent and to see a guy bring a dog in some stage of heat to a dog park. It was a clash of discomforts inside me.

The previous month, Tom and I had gotten Toby neutered. We'd agreed to do that when we bought him from Dana Loud of Mirabelle Labs, as she tried to control her breeding lines; and we'd agreed with each other that the world and its many rescue organizations needed no more unexpected or unwanted puppies. A friend of ours was adamantly against neutering, but I felt that it was a misguided projection onto a dog, one that could result in homeless litters and doom a city dog surrounded by a community of neutered dogs to a complicated social existence. It's the kind of projection that might have caused the Night of the White Dog, when Hayley, Nash, and I saw a lost dog disappear into the darkness of the park, no person to be with. That was the night Officer Marv refused to help.

We'd left Toby at the vet the day of his operation, worried about the idea of surgery and anesthesia; and then, when we picked him up that evening, we giggled about how woozy he was as he got into the car. He was walking with a loosey-goosey step and he looked like a happy little junkie, his still-too-big snout nodding every now and then. Like so much having to do with Toby, it seemed, the experience ended with sweetness.

But this humping thing was a new twist, one that Tom, who never went to the park, didn't have to deal with.

A few days after the first Zelda incident, Zelda and Nick were at the park again, and exactly the same situation played out. Toby went for Zelda, and Nick grabbed Toby too aggressively and gave me a snarl. Hayley and Nash followed me over to get Toby, and they heard him go off on me.

"You *know* what he wants. Just take him away. He's a bad dog. This is not right." He went on and on, too loudly.

He was so angry about humping, there was no room for me to be apologetic about Toby. I took my boy away, but I was frustrated.

Part of me still really understood Nick and his anger. I didn't like it when dogs humped Toby, so I knew that uneasy feeling of watching your own puppy get his or her first taste of social jockeying in the animal world. It's a jarring and disruptive event in your early days with a dog. But I was thrown by Nick's hostility, especially since Zelda was still in the last stage of her heat. He was bringing far too much affect to the situation, as if unaware that dogs are dogs. He acted as though this were some kind of boxing situation governed by the Marquess of Queensberry rules and we weren't playing fair.

As I walked away with Hayley and Nash, Toby on the leash, he was still yelling about how I *knew* what Toby wanted to do. We three looked at one another with a creeped-out roll of our eyes. He was not sympathetic.

Two weeks later, on a Saturday in late April, Nick came up to me. There was an evening potluck supper at the park with some of the dog owners at the wooden picnic tables under the willows. Margo had called it a celebration of spring, and I decided to go.

There were pastries and cookies on the tables, some chicken wings with thick barbecue sauce on them, and a few bottles of wine and plastic cups. I was hanging out near the food, making sure Toby didn't actually climb onto the picnic table from the bench where he was perched, sniffing, flexing his neck and full snout toward the chicken wings, when Nick came up to me.

"I'm sorry about that whole thing the other day," he said, definitely in his cups but with a look of sincerity in his eyes. "I took the wrong approach, and I was too pushy. Sorry about that. I don't want to get Zelda fixed, but I may have to do it."

I was touched by his honesty and his willingness to apologize. It's easy to be an asshole; it's hard to apologize for being an asshole. He did it in public, so a few people heard, and it was a nice moment. A stranger saying "I'm sorry" to another stranger in front of others was poignant.

Hayley and Nash were at that potluck supper and they saw my exchange with Nick and were impressed that he had come forth like that. We were all expressing kudos.

And I wanted that to be the end of the story, the lesson of forgiveness, but there was yet another scene—there always is at the park. The very next Saturday, there was a large group of people and a lot of big and small dogs tumbling together, and instantly Toby spotted Zelda in the crowd and went after her. I saw it coming. He was in hot pursuit again, and Nick was looking flinchy and concerned.

But then in a dramatic detour, Toby veered off for another dog, a young Catahoula. Toby was after Kramer and not Zelda! Meanwhile, Zelda ran elsewhere, chasing a Boston terrier with a ball, ignored. And Toby and Kramer played. He didn't want to hump Kramer so much as tackle and roll with him. But I didn't want to take the chance, with Nick so close by, and I prematurely led him away on his leash.

And as Toby and I passed Nick, I heard him spitefully, almost gleefully, saying to another owner, "That dog humps three hundred and sixty-five days a year! He's awful."

Did he know I was right there, hearing every word? I thought so. It was too weird, hearing someone coldly trashing your dog, and for no reason. When I heard him say "He's awful," I felt as parental as I've ever felt. So I went up to him and said, "You really don't have to say that," and he looked at me as if I were a fool.

"Jesus, it's my dog," I said.

It just seemed so ridiculous, to openly demonize a dog, especially such a peaceful dog. I pulled Toby away without looking back.

And that's where it ended, with two grown men standing as far as possible from each other that spring, in the same park but always at opposite ends of the crowd. Toby's urge to hump Zelda had stopped as quickly as it had started, but our two dogs still engaged with each other over rubber balls and chases, regardless of their owners' tightened jaws and stubborn ignorance.

There are people, alas, whom you just don't click with, but you learn to coexist with them. Now Nick was one of those people for me. Saul needed to get a smile from every person in his path, or his day was destroyed, but most of us had stronger defense systems.

One guy, Brent, had an impenetrable defense system that was nondiscriminatory. The owner of a black pit bull named Burma, he avoided the people and dogs at Amory, always keeping to the periphery of the pack. He was proud of Burma, maybe too much so. You'd see him on the hill with her on the leash, and he looked like a lonely guy. He had a round, bald head that always seemed to be looking down, a strip of hair around his ears, a furrowed forehead, and dark eyes that expressed impatience. He seemed a little Dickensian, as if there was a family secret there, an old house and cobwebs and a faked death certificate maybe. Burma was older, and her solid body waddled a bit, a coallike cannon ambling forward from sniff to sniff. You could see her nipples underneath.

I watched them that April, and I kept wanting to say hello. I'd warmed up to the friendliness of the dog people I'd been getting to know, and I was assuming that if you weren't a Charlotte, you were probably trustworthy. I was starting to approach people with no entrée, appropriating some of Margo's extroversion.

And I didn't want Brent to think I was afraid of pit bulls, or prejudiced against them. When someone showed up at the park with a pit bull, you frequently saw people move on with their dogs. You could see anxiety in their faces, remnant memories of those newspaper articles about pit bull attacks and jaws of steel. Those who didn't slowly but surely walk away would sometimes go overboard in letting the owner know they had no preset notions about pit bulls, like me. Either way, it was an issue.

So one day, I climbed the hill, with Toby behind me, and walked up to Brent and Burma. I said hello.

"She looks like she's in good shape," I said.

He looked at me, then looked back down. He couldn't be bothered.

"Is she a full pit bull?" I asked.

"No," he said without looking up. "She's an American Staffordshire terrier." That was a more formal name for the same dog—the name without the baggage.

He snubbed me to the second degree. It was too bad. I wanted to try harder to get him to talk, but he was not going to stop. Maybe if I'd had a pit bull, too, we could have had a moment together. Burma just kept sniffing onward, oblivious.

The owners of pit bulls, it seems, have a very distinct journey with their dogs. People are afraid of them; issues of trust are in the air. Some, like Brent, are very aware of the public perception. You could see the battle on his face; he seemed weary of the fight.

crushing

It was a happy collision between my TV world and my park world. I started to think about the way all the dogs that I was meeting at the park seemed to have celebrity doubles. Sooner or later, you'd figure out which star matched a particular dog's essence, just as you'd eventually figure out the nature of the dog-owner caravan. To me, Annabel, a seventy-pound black-and-white female mutt, who'd have nothing to do with Toby, was Audrey Hepburn in the "Ascot Gavotte" scene from *My Fair Lady*. She had dainty white gloves on her paws, and a slightly anxious bearing. And everyone knew she just might let loose with a giant, socially unacceptable howl when overexcited.

After getting to know Bertha, I saw Nash's golden retriever as Grace Kelly—reserved and elegant. "I can live with that," Nash said. I'd been told that Toby, so blond and fit, was Matthew McConaughey, but to me, he was a young Gary Cooper— maybe not as pretty as McConaughey, but more classic, for sure. Sometimes when Toby saw a dog across Amory field, a vague figure to me, he'd crouch and reenact the standoff from

High Noon, all trembling stillness and awareness, waiting to see who'd move first.

And Nellie, Lucinda's giant fawn Great Dane, was Allison Janney from *The West Wing.* She was a tan, horsey gal with a dry sense of humor. Her head was large in proportion to her body, a quality that fit the celebrity-double theory perfectly. Celebrities, it turns out, frequently have giant heads when you see them in person. For years, I did celebrity interviews for the *Globe,* most of them in New York, and it was not uncommon for me to walk into a hotel room and be greeted by a cantaloupe on a stick. Was it from all that mugging for cameras, which somehow overly built up facial muscles? Did having a metaphorical big head somehow eventually take literal form? Or was it that obsessive low-carb Hollywood dieting and exercise kept necks and bodies so lean that heads simply appeared oversized—an optical illusion?

I'd gawk in awe at the gorgeous, tall Nellie with her giant head and her long, skinny legs, trotting around the park with a syncopated grace, her will moving a few paces ahead of her body, rocking her head forward to *just . . . get . . . there.* When she'd try to stop, she was even more perfectly imprecise, and far less intentional, a train wreck of legs and drooly jowls and googly eyes. It was like a cartoon dustup, with "Thump!" and "Thwack!" and "Kaboom!" and, miraculously, no serious damage. When Nellie set her Great Dane sights on something, or someone, or some handsome George Clooney–looking mutt, she got there, and then some. It was a love crash.

———

Dogs, with their uncomplicated expressiveness, can make us more loving. It's corny to think that dogs can bring out the best in their humans, that they can be our teachers; it's embroidered on countless pillows and footstools that eventually find their way to the stalls in rural antiques stores. But still, I'd succumbed. After decades of distance, I'd found dogs and love with Tom and was becoming willing to put down my guns and let strangers cross the borders of my property. Hayley had found dogs long ago, but she was still holding on to her rifle; it was slung across her chest, just in case, while she was motioning Drew in.

That spring, Hayley frequently spent her off days—Monday and Tuesday—with her parents in Vermont, despite the fact that they made Stewie stay in their breezeway. She loved to complain to me about her father, a retired insurance salesman who picked food off her plate and laughed at her furry winter boots, saying they were for "Hollywood winters," but she clearly idolized him. She'd cycle through her anger about her father's behavior, and I'd sympathize, and then she'd remind me of how funny he was and how he'd taught her to love history.

I increasingly had the sense that not making progress with Drew was becoming untenable for her, as she had to decide what to do with her life after the semester ended. She wanted to be a teacher and grow up, become a wife, stare down her mother's condescension about her being single; Drew had become her ticket. Her fantasy was that Drew was ready to give up the bars and clubs, just as she was, that he liked forward women, that he was ready to embrace personality over breasts.

"I really think he's the kind of guy who's tired of being a player," she'd say to me with conviction when I hinted at his escapades. "He's ready to retire. And I want to be his retirement benefit. . . ."

Maybe she knows better than I do, I thought. But the reality contradicted her at every turn as he dodged her requests for help in getting her iPod to work in her car, and as he ignored her multiple invitations to him and me—but really him—to visit the restaurant where she worked. He was a handsome, single, straight male in his early thirties, and he was into juggling women. He was going to be a guy's guy for years to come, and he preferred slightly passive women to someone as formidable as Hayley. "Entourage" was his fantasy—he'd told me that ten times. For all her fearlessness and wisdom, that was something Hayley didn't understand.

All she saw was Drew's devotion to Chester, the way he got a little glassy-eyed when talking about his buddy.

"I love my guy," he'd say sometimes, using the word *love* unself-consciously. Each time Chester breathlessly brought that yellow ball back to Drew, over and over for an hour or more, the pleasure registered anew on his face. When it poured, Drew was out there with Chester just the same, both seeming water-resistant. When Chester had health issues involving mysterious lumps, Drew was a mess, a little boy in a Cro-Magnon body, sweet Timmy fretting over Lassie. Tears welling, he seemed so open to connection. Hayley was encouraged.

On days when Hayley wasn't around, he'd still talk to me about the women in his life—the ex-girlfriend who still pined for him, the woman he was hooking up with and then dodging, the disinterested lawyer on the West Coast he was driven to pursue. His BlackBerry was always buzzing with date scheduling and postdate analysis with his friends. But he was mum about sex whenever Hayley was around; it was guy talk. He was a prepubescent boy when it came to Chester, but he was a teen boy when it came to girls. In *Archie* America, he sat comfortably on the spectrum between an Archie and a Reggie, a little more toward the Reggie end of things.

And then Hayley began a last-ditch effort. Drew's reserve toward her pushed her into it. She started bringing stories of her after-work parties to the park, as if to inspire Drew, to push him into action. Her waitress job was sweeping her into decadence, she bragged. Lots of sexcapades. Did she want Drew to get turned on, or was she inviting him to rescue her?

One Saturday morning, she told us that she'd not yet been to sleep, that she'd hooked up with a fellow waiter after getting drunk on tequila at a few bars, that they'd had sex on a couch at the Beacon Hill apartment of someone she didn't know. The guy meant nothing to her, but it had been So Much Fun. She had that third-wind craziness in her eyes, and her hands seemed to be shaking as she sipped her giant Dunkin' Donuts coffee.

"I can still taste the Cuervo," she said.

She was, I would say, despite her audacious affect, despite her bold purple hoodie, completely unprotected. For an hour, I watched her try to reel in Drew's interest. It was May.

Drew was unimpressed, as always. If she'd been a guy, he'd have had plenty to say about a night of carousing. I was rooting for her, hoping the two people I liked so much would link up, thinking I might be part of their origin story. But Drew maintained his same old smirk with her, the smirk that refused to sink a thousand maiden voyages into hope. She was a blip on his screen; he was her obsession, her psychic home page.

She'd always asked me if I thought Drew was even slightly interested, or how she might snag him, or at least get him on an out-of-the-park date; but after that day, she stopped. She knew that, after her hungover performance, she'd failed. And I stopped mentioning it, too. She'd opened herself up to the wrong guy; she'd used her beautiful persistence and resilience in service of an unavailable case. She'd once told me that Stewie was her role model, that she admired the way injury never seemed to get him down, the way he never held grudges. But after Drew, she seemed a little more cautious, a little less "Stewelicious," the nickname she'd invented for her boy.

I'd been too protective of my heart for decades; Hayley had, too, in her own brash way. Dogs off the leash at the park can court and spark one another in an instant, so directly, so openly; it's not that simple for us.

At times, Nellie would sit alone on the field and chew a stick, just a big Great Dane with a large head and a tiny treat, but she was ever ready to abandon that prize if another dog wanted to play. At even the slightest hint of interest, she'd hoist herself up and shake her head as if to whinny, drool flying.

Lucinda and I would stand and laugh at Nellie's mustering of energy. Her gangling legs would reposition themselves underneath her, all in one suspended moment, and soon she was striding across the baseball diamond, chasing down a little pug with a Russell Crowe face, like a giant jalopy trailing a Mini Cooper.

Watching a Great Dane tear after a stout, handbag-size pug is broad physical comedy, but also a sweet portrait of resolve. Because as soon as Nellie caught up to her target, inevitably her target turned on a dime, eluding her, leaving her in her own dust, regrouping for still more pursuit in another direction. Her objects of desire—sometimes even Labs—ran under her, too, escaping.

One morning, out of the blue, Nellie was after Toby, and Toby only, like the dawning of a new relationship. It was one sharp turn after another, a series of Z and V shapes across the field, with Nellie never giving up, right until she finally reached him, or, more likely, until he let her reach him. And in that moment of breathless respite, on their first date, when they were both in the same spot, stopped together, panting, she took the only action that made sense to her. And it was the most natural thing in the world: She sat on him. And he stayed put.

summer

departures

I was sorry to see Hayley move out of Boston after her gradua-
tion, during the annual student summer migration that leaves
the roads tranquil and filled with parking opportunities. Suddenly, Commonwealth Avenue was an unclogged artery.

It caught me by surprise, the amount of connection I'd felt
with her in such a brief time. I'd never seen her outside the
boundaries of our neighborhood, and most of our confidences
were made in an open field, surrounded by other people, draped
in dirty, unhooked leashes and carrying balls in our pockets.
But that cathartic quality of dog-park conversation, as your dogs
stirred up honesty and confidences with their obviousness and
their naked temperaments, could take you a long way in a short
time.

I'd seen her in the morning, her long hair wet and smelling
like citrus, holding her Dunkin' Donuts cup, and then in the
evening, more giggly, gearing up for a seminar or a shift at the
restaurant, again with the coffee. I'd seen her kiss Stewie on
his wet nose while pulling at his ears more times than I could
count. We'd been for walks around that field over and over

again, with Nash and Margo and others, Toby and Stewie trailing us. We'd been through the Drew story together, I'd seen Stewie get bitten by a German shepherd, and I'd helped her nurse a serious hangover or two. One day, we'd smoked a joint together at the park and laughed out loud like maniacs— that was the day she'd told me she wanted to get a tattoo of Margo's face right on her arm so she could look at it and always feel that mixture of chaos and humor.

"I want her being imprinted on my soul," she said, while I cackled at the thought.

First she was dropping clues about a job search, and about her sister's small apartment in Brooklyn, and how she might be able to work in the city and still meet Stewie's needs if her sister was willing to help out. I offered to look into dog sitters and doggy day care locations in Brooklyn, but I could see she already had a plan. She'd tell me, ventriloquially, that Stewie was going to miss Toby if they left town.

" 'I'll call you on the doggy hot line, Toby,' " she'd say in Stewie's voice.

" 'Well, I'll sure look forward to that, Mr. Stewart,' " I'd have Toby reply.

And then, before I quite realized it, there were good-byes and extra cookies for Toby and other dogs. And then there were Facebook friend requests.

It was a microcosmic part of the dog park, the way people came and went. Sometimes someone you liked just vanished, stopped coming, and you knew you'd never see that person again in the same casual way. You'd run into them in the market and awkwardly ask after each other's dogs. You'd had a special daily bond that you couldn't easily conjure up or re-create on a cell phone. I'd seen how Hayley was ambivalent about cell phones and knew she was an in-the-moment type of person. I'd felt that kind of loss, to a lesser degree, when Ky disappeared from the scene. Despite his poop-rebel issues, I'd liked seeing him around. He was a character, and there were a few weeks there when we were buddies, before his final episodes.

Often, it seemed as though the park people were the ensemble of a TV sitcom, *The Office* or *How I Met Your Mother* or *Scrubs* or *Seinfeld,* where different types of people intermingled—at work, in a bar, in an apartment—on a regular basis. It was as if my life of endlessly watching story lines from afar on TV was merging with living story lines in the park, with some synchronicity between the two. Just as all dogs had celebrity doubles, all the park people seemed to have sitcom doubles. Talky Noreen, for example, with her nonstop geekery, was Sheldon on *The Big Bang Theory.* Now I was the removed guy letting down his guard—Jim from *The Office,* with his cynical eyes looking straight at the camera, or chilly, defensive Miranda warming up on *Sex and the City.* I was Rob Petrie from *The Dick Van Dyke Show,* in a way, the man who was like a father to me, with a life that included writing, television, and a few Buddys and Sallys.

It all had comic resolution. Margo was the kooky rare bird of a neighbor or boss who popped up on every sitcom and was lovable and wise. Maybe she was Mrs. Garrett on *The Facts of Life.* She and Travis were great comic relief, cosmic and untethered. Nash was Hawkeye Pierce from *M*A*S*H,* with his constant wry asides and an instinct for what really mattered. I'd think of *Will & Grace* and be reminded of Hayley, as we bickered and yet knew each other too well. We had a kind of coded language that strangers sometimes couldn't understand, with our references to Cell Phone Lady and my pathetic ball-throwing abilities. Or she'd make me think of Elaine from *Seinfeld,* maybe mixed with some Dee on *It's Always Sunny in Philadelphia.*

It took me a few weeks to stop looking for Hayley after her departure. Like the TV ensembles, the park people saw their park wives and park husbands more than their friends and spouses out in the world. The regulars learned one another's special traits and some of their secrets. We read one another's weaknesses, teased as a sign of affection, and noticed absences—classic sitcom behavior. We were at the *Cheers* bar, and the dogs were the booze that loosened us up.

Suddenly, in a shocking turn, Chester died. Hayley was gone, which is probably a good thing. She might have seen the tragedy, and Drew's grief, as an opportunity to try with him again. His sadness might have led her back to thinking that his tenderness toward dogs somehow meant he could be her sensitive boyfriend.

It happened really fast. Chester was sluggish, Drew had mentioned a few times, and you could see Chester panting more heavily during their fetching sessions. More lumps emerged, Drew said, and soon there was a diagnosis of lymphoma, and, by late June, Chester was gone. It was strange to imagine that the athletic ridgeback mix obsessed with that yellow ball was no longer doing his proud running.

Drew fell apart. His grief was constant, and you could see

the heaviness in his walk. He refused to come to the park. "I just can't even walk by there anymore," he said, surprised at the strength of his feelings about the place blocks from his apartment that he'd once visited every day. Tom and I had him over for dinner one night shortly after Chester died, and he looked lost as Toby danced around him, demanding play, unaware of sorrow.

"I will never do it again," he told me and Tom.

"Wait and see," I said, not wanting to be disrespectful but trying to be optimistic. I was feeling more and more like it was possible to survive grief, that it was a price worth paying for love, that it made you aware of the present. I'd always thought I had been ruined by the death of my father, that I was so much less alive and complete than my friends who'd never experienced loss and tragedy. My heart had a fissure in it; theirs were still whole. But I was starting to accept that an awareness of death wasn't a disadvantage or a weakness. Once you've been through a loss, you better understand life.

This tall, muscle-bound man in his early thirties with the rugged face of a hockey player was thrown in a boyish way. It was the first time Drew had found himself deep inside loss. He'd read about it, and he'd known people who'd lost loved ones—Lucinda, for example, to whom he'd taken a frozen pizza after her little daughter died. And on some level, everyone knows loss is coming when you take in a dog; you know you're probably going to outlive him or her, and have to say good-bye, like it or not. You know that dog ownership, dog love, is a setup. But nonetheless, he was knocked over.

Every day with Toby, I still thought about losing him,

188 • matthew gilbert

fended off the lurking anticipatory grief that had been my shadow brother for decades. It was still following me, that Harold persona. But now I tried to let the awareness of Toby's short time here help me savor him. That was a big part of our caravan, his showing me the daily, mundane building of attachment. Toby was irresistible, became my buddy, took me to the park, and showed me how to forget the Big Spoiler. You have to know and accept the inevitable ending and then block the hell out of it. You have to know it and then deny it. You have to intervene when your thoughts turn to the inescapability of loss, the certain good-bye; you have to keep them in perspective. You have to force yourself to trade feelings of dread for the energy of the present tense, the panting dog who you can so easily make so intensely happy. I was letting Toby prod me out of my commitment to the dark truths that I'd been so wedded to.

Drew had ignored the inevitable easily and successfully for the eight years of Chester's life, blocked out the future each time Chester dropped that ball at his feet. Next time around, with his next dog—and I was sure he would have a next dog—he would have to work a lot harder to forget the end of the story.

Drew had a collection of pictures of Chester in his apartment, a shrine on his rickety wooden kitchen table with framed and warped photos, and they were lovely. That prancing brown dog, all across his life, smiling and sleeping and jumping and being a sports nerd. It was a happy existence I saw, a dog active and goofy, loving and loved. His shiny ridged back always seemed to be in a state of excitement. There were lots of shots of him at the park, the yellow ball in his teeth.

I stopped by Drew's place, looked affectionately at the pictures, my first close-up dog death, and felt a respect for his openness to grief. His black eyelashes were in little clumps around his eyes from crying. Toby walked around Drew's kitchen, sniffing, while we talked about what it was like to be so inescapably miserable about something most people would dismiss. Drew and I talked about how so many people in his life didn't identify with dog grief, and that the dog-park people were giving him the most acknowledgment and kindness. I recalled Lucinda's praise for how the park people rallied around her. There was something exquisite about this pack of people—a few who played rough, a few who were learning, but still a bunch of good ones.

There was another departure that June, of one of the park's supporting players.

Inevitably, the park became a haven for people who didn't quite make it in the culture at large. The randomness of the park population—the way people breezed through in suits and skirts on their way to work, or with bags of fast food to eat while sitting at the picnic tables, or with blankets to make a shelter for a few nights—meant there were surprises every day. The pack of freaks was an ever-changing one, with cameo appearances (Claude, with her *Macbeth*) and guest arcs (Ky the Zen Shit Strewer) that mingled with the regular cast every week. The meandering Saul was a recurring character, with a circular plot line that had a little comedy and a little pathos as his last bits of memory disappeared.

Some of the guest stars tested everyone around them, just as the needy dogs did—the passive-aggressive Charlotte, the reverse snob pitt bull owner Brent, or the spiky Marcella, the judgmental lady with a bouffant, whom I'd met early on and who didn't like TV, people who talked about TV, or, it seemed, dogs. They were thorns, even while they sometimes made life interesting. The Buck Lady—no one knew her name, but her dog was Buck—often stood alone in the Amory field, scrubbing her face without soap and water, or dancing like an addled belly dancer, or talking too angrily about the government's "imperialistic push." Maybe schizophrenic, maybe just super quirky, she ignored her sweet black-and-white mutt, who was a magnet to mud. When Buck pooped in the middle of the field, crouching for all to see, sniffing peacefully at the air, no one had the nerve to alert the Buck Lady. Conversation might ensue.

But Saul was one of the more amusing and beloved fringe characters. Occasionally, I'd overlap with dog people who came to the park at different hours than Nash, Margo, and I did—we all thought we were *the* park regulars, but, in fact, there were a number of sitcoms running during the day—and they'd mention Saul, the wandering Odysseus, or Noreen, the Chatty Cathy. These people were legendary in the world of the dog park, many of them the people I'd dismissed early on. Margo, I now loved. Noreen, too. She was a great barrier-breaking presence, and her worship of TV was endearing to me. That guy who'd talked to me about his estranged wife and his dying dog, Maya, during one of my first days at the park, he knew it was a place where he could tell a story that wouldn't come back to haunt him. "They are better than Beings," Emily Dickinson wrote in a letter about her companions, which were the hills, the "sundown," and a dog. "They are better than

Beings—because they know—but do not tell." The park could have that same confidential quality.

Abruptly, Saul's daily park life came to a close. For a week running, he didn't come to the park, and he hadn't mentioned any kind of vacation or hospital visit to anyone. We didn't see his car creeping into a parking space, or him doing his loops.

Nash finally tracked down Saul's phone number and called. The news was gloomy. We knew that Saul's brother had not been ready to stop Saul from driving; such a decision is always hard to make. And so he'd finally gotten in a minor traffic accident in a nearby Beacon Street neighborhood, his brother explained to Nash, and had left the scene without quite realizing that he'd dented another car. He'd probably felt a small bump when he was backing up, and then just moved forward and continued on. And he was probably on his way to the park when the mishap occurred; the park was really his only destination at that point. The police got involved, went to his house, and met with his brother, and Saul had had his license taken away.

It was a good thing. He really shouldn't have been on the roads. But he was gone from the park, and his brother had mentioned the possibility of putting Saul into an assisted living facility during the phone call. We started missing having to answer his same questions over and over again, telling him this was Toby, a yellow Lab, very gentle. We were his daily linchpin, and so were other park dog people who gathered at other times. We all dodged him when we weren't in the mood and indulged him when we were. Sweet old guy.

We'd caught part of the tail end of his life, lived that out with him, been his farewell party.

haters

As a dog-park person in the Boston area, you were by definition a little bit notorious. It was laughable, given the relative peace and calm in the parks. There was local controversy about your lifestyle, both for and against you, compassionate and cold. We faced regular harassment by cops—the puffed-up Officer Marv, in particular, with his verbal caveman's club—and also by rabidly antidog neighbors. Our issues and our right to use the parks were debated in the newspapers and at town meetings, in the same way gay marriage has been picked over publicly by those whose lives it doesn't really affect. Just our existence polarized other people, no matter how ordinary we were out on that grassy field with our dogs, no matter that we paid our taxes like everyone else, and it felt weird.

Sometimes, a baseball coach or a jogger would go off on one of us about our awful dogs at Amory, which, if he or she was looking at Toby, Bertha, or Travis, panting, with balls in their mouths, would be a comic disconnect. How odd to see anyone look askance at Bertha, who had Grace Kelly as her celebrity double, who was so ladylike and yet so passionate as she knocked your hand for more head patting and scratching. Toby and Travis were all about play, and they could irritate humans trying to play peacefully with a ball or a Frisbee, but Bertha, she was all love.

"Give me your e-mail address," one angry man at the park yelled at me after Toby had started to pursue the soccer ball he was practicing with.

"Not gonna happen," I said, putting Toby on the leash and pulling him away while his body and mind leaned hard toward the ball.

As news outlets explained in countless features, the United States had developed into a "nation of dog lovers," with dog reality shows, dog sections in bookstores, a crazy number of dog groomers and day-care sitters, and some remarkable statistics involving billions of dollars spent on dog food, veterinary bills, and toys—even in the middle of tricky financial times. As facile pop psychologists—including me, no doubt, in some Animal Planet TV review or another—were noting, when our material aspirations seemed limited during economic downturns, we turned back to our home lives for satisfaction. Our dogs were anchors on the den rug, holding the family pack together, releasing stress and softening differences just by being there. Also, as I'd definitely experienced, the more isolated we were by our virtual illusions of connection, the more the simple directness and proximity of a dog pleased. No buttons to tap, no distance in the way, no protective detachment in place, no glass; there he or she was, playful, wry, grouchy, present.

But there were plenty of haters, too, the Frank Burnses and Hot Lips Houlihan, whose mission was to belittle and disempower city dog owners, to keep us and our dogs from going off the leash together.

Every urban area had them, the haters, who lived to shut down a nearby doggy wonderland because it somehow threatened their boundaries. Rather than choosing to work with us to control barking and apprehend the poop delinquents and poop rebels, they quickly retreated to a default position of harsh opposition. Certainly there were problems to address in every dog park, but were any of those problems insurmountable? We all needed to do battle against the Charlottes, to keep life as safe as possible within the gates of the garden.

In my neighborhood, there were actually two parks with off-leash dog hours, Winthrop as well as Amory. They were quite different. Amory was picturesque, open, with a view of the sunset and the rising moon. It was the little paradise where your dog could run in ever-bigger loops around you, where Toby got his puppy energy out with endless beelines across the field and back. Amory had become my second home, as you know, but Winthrop was a valuable alternative. Winthrop was smaller and fenced in, a city block surrounded by brown-brick apartment buildings and a kiddie playground with swing sets and rosebushes. It was a subplot. It was a fat postage stamp, like so many urban dog parks in this country, where the dogs ran in denser circles and dog crashes were not uncommon. It was an ideal location for people whose dogs tended to run away or chase cars. If you'd just gotten a rescue dog and you weren't sure if he or she would take off toward some perceived prey, or to find some vaguely remembered home, Winthrop was a protected testing ground, contained but thriving, especially on Saturday mornings.

It turned out that there was a man living in an apartment adjacent to Winthrop, who could easily see down to the dogs playing and the people mingling in the park. Sitting in his living room or standing at his kitchen sink, this abutter with the gray aura glared onto the field and seethed. I never met him, but I felt as though I knew him too well, as the park people began to talk about the constant complaints that summer that he'd registered against us with the local Parks and Recreation Commission. He's immune to the innocence of the dogs, this guy, I thought. He disliked the people who loved dogs, scorned the playful, hierarchyless mess that stirred right below him. Each whoop of glee, each howl from a loquacious beagle named Murphy, each yelled-out "Come" command by a frustrated owner, each tumble of laughs, was probably like water torture to him. He wanted control, quiet.

From a distance, it seemed, he cast a hunched-shouldered shadow over the park people. He spent his spare hours counting barks—Can you imagine counting barks? Do you do that in iambs, stanzas, or paragraphs?—and tracking fugitive poops with his binoculars, like FCC executives studying boob shots and expletives on the latest televised awards show. He became an expert on the dangers of dog shit, and while I don't believe he'd ever spotted Ky and his brown eyes and his philosophical approach to poop, he saw visions of a man like Ky in his gnawing fantasies. He rallied a few other neighbors by sharing his hellish vision: dogs of all kinds slobbering on and nipping at children and decadent owners celebrating frenzied animal behavior, laughing as they left dog shit in the grass for kids to step in.

Maybe this man even rubbed Purell on his hands at the very thought of all this commotion.

Summer weekend mornings at Winthrop could be sunny adventures, like a tribal reunion of different breeds of dogs and people. No one was trying to keep his pressed pants clean for the workday ahead, the dogs chased and flirted and panted close by one another, and the humans, especially the Amory regulars who traveled a few blocks west, found themselves talking to strangers. It was a spot of eternity, with dogs as the liaisons. The circus was in town for a Saturday moment.

Some regulars would bring family members we'd only heard tell of. Bette, it turned out, wasn't just a character in Nash's stories about his family life, the one he tried to outpsych to do the dishes; she was his knockout wife, who clearly had her own elaborate connection with Bertha. "I like to hike with her," Bette said, reminding me a little of Tom and his preference for one-on-one time with Toby. They walked together along the Charles River, without the interpersonal complications of the park. Bette and Bertha were a pair of fair-haired twins, a caravan of compounded beauty. I could see that at home, they had Nash beat; they were the lovely power source in the house.

Noreen lived near Winthrop Park, and she loved to go there on weekends, to spring her material on new people. And there was a regular Noreen of Winthrop, too, who talked a lot but was lovely and vulnerable and looking for connection. When I'd open the steel gate for Toby and unhook him, he'd run in with extra focus, since all the people and dogs were so close together.

I'm convinced that the beginning of the end of Winthrop as

a dog park occurred on a hot Saturday morning in late July
when a bulldog Web site organized a bulldog "meetup" there.

Meetups were celebrations where a crew of similar-looking
dogs got together; but they struck fear and loathing in the
hearts of some dog-park people. Meetups tended to intrude on
the diversity and randomness of park life. As the owners of one
breed bonded, turning away from the mutts and the various
breeds surrounding them, frowning on the bold interlopers
who trotted into their club without a membership, they could
be cliquey. They'd dominate and split the scene.

The day of the bulldog meetup at Winthrop was my first in-
depth exposure to bulldogs. They were everywhere, these giant,
rubbery, swollen pencil erasers bouncing off one another, wad-
dling like squat businessmen, drool leaking from their gummy
mouths. Even Toby seemed a little weirded-out, aware he was
surrounded by a small army of Winston Churchills.

Around noon, the sun incandescent, the breathless Toby,
having played a round of fetch with me, trotted over to the
group water bowl for a slurp, and even he, a Lab who snacks
on branches and goose poop, refused to drink. The viscous
water, lapped at and slobbered into by the many hot bulldogs,
sat before him, still and ropy, slime soup. Toby pulled his head
back from the bowl like he did when I tried to wipe booger
from his eyes.

"You kiddin' me," he said with his eyes.

It amused me that the bulldog meetup was a display of everything Americans held to be most ugly. These dogs, and there
were probably fifteen of them that day, had every problem that
health and beauty magazines devote themselves to solving.
They panted, they sagged, they had no necks, their jaws jutted,

they had tiny teeth, and they had short legs. No matter their age, their faces were crinkled with wrinkles like the older, world-weary W. H. Auden.

One portly man in shorts up to his belly button, his shirt tucked in, stood panting, watching his guy, Burger, stand there panting. The man was overheated; the bulldog was, too. Their visual caravan was instantly clear: a pair of matching oval bookends, Wimpy and Wimpy, two Newmans from *Seinfeld*. And together they shared the perimeter, far left fielders, off to the side of the action even in a park lined with their compadres.

Toby and I approached and, as always at the dog park, I asked the guy his dog's name and age. Burger was four, and his bulging eyes quickly became intent on me, as if I was about to give him a treat, or maybe a light for his cigar. And, as I knelt with my eyes at his level, he struck me as a funny little comedian—a miniature Jackie Mason, maybe. He took the cookie and chomped it in my face, bloodshot eyes never leaving mine. I patted him, laughing.

"Bulldogs are funny," I said, standing up. "You can't help but smile at them. They're like this joke in motion, you know?"

Burger's owner, Fred, straddled the fence between mystified and offended. He blinked at me. "No, I don't." Fred was not going to help me out. "I have no idea what you're talking about," he said, now blinking more aggressively, sweat coating his forehead, arms folded across his chest.

"I meant it in a nice way, you know, as in 'I think bulldogs are fun.'"

My explanation was pointless. He gave me a stone face and looked off behind me; he was done with me.

Yeah, Fred had busted me. I was not yet a bulldog convert. I didn't get the warm and fuzzies over bulldogs, although I was beginning to feel the appeal of their stumpiness and their humor. He didn't need to deal with a bulldog newbie.

But he got me thinking. What is ugly? Toby tried to play with Burger, bowing down at him, and Burger looked at Toby with infinite patience and gave a few little four-legged hops. He was just a funny, porky guy, and I couldn't help but smile at him. The bulldog meetup wasn't a conventionally pretty sight, but it was a gorgeous sight. People compared and cooed over their dogs; there was a whole lot of joy in the air. Bulldogs! And joy—that corny, embarrassing, overused noun—was the bottom line at the dog park.

It turned out that the short words could be pretty good: *joy, play, talk.*

Enough joy, alas, to alert that neighbor who was allergic to disorder.

Winthrop at its most crowded reached maybe ten dogs; on bulldog day, there were about twenty-five dogs in all. The hater above the park looked out of his window and saw too many dogs, and too many ugly dogs. And he pulled out his camera. And then he pulled out his notepad in a spiral of negative energy.

It was soon after that day that the town meetings included Winthrop Park and dogs on the agenda. His complaint became a cause for the antidog pockets in the neighborhood, and the pro-dog forces organized. There were daily clashes. One day, a woman with a kerchief on her head walked outside the fence along Pleasant Street yelling shrilly, "This PARK isn't for DOGS and their SHIT." Was she a woman off her meds or a quiet neighbor driven to primitive expression?

Officer Marv became even more persistently offensive than usual, ticketing the owners of barking dogs and checking registration tags as if he were playing Monopoly and collecting property cards in his greedy hands. The state of Massachusetts could be under attack, thieves could be holding a parade down Beacon Street, and Marv would still be watching the dog park, on the lookout for the next dog-owning scofflaw.

He was part of a sitcom, our Marv; he was the punch line.

Gradually, when you went to Winthrop, you began to feel like it was a prison yard and your every move was being watched and judged. By the final days, you didn't even want to be there; all anyone could do was talk angrily about what was happening to Winthrop, how unfair it was. It was a bummer, standing around complaining helplessly.

Ultimately, Winthrop was officially deemed unfriendly to dogs. No more dog hours. That lone crusader had won. Below him sat an empty field, available for kids' soccer practice and the occasional picnic, manicured and sedate, the graveyard of a few good times.

clash of innocents

Despite Winthrop's demise, Amory was still going strong. We all spent hours every day there, in showers and on perfect blue-sky afternoons.

Under the green and heavy weeping willows of July, packs of dogs and owners would huddle away from the rain and the sun amid the smells of freshly mown grass. The wooden picnic tables continued their distinguished aging process, with Toby sitting proudly on them whenever he could, while I kept watch for Marv. On hot days, Bertha would sit panting, elegant in her furs, making an occasional fetch when Nash felt like throwing her ball, while Travis, always hyper, would scamper after anything round that came into view.

We watched the town lawn mowers cross the field in mysterious patterns, ripping up forsaken tennis balls and leaving the fragments to sink into the dirt for future archaeologists.

A daily minyan of dog people, we'd stand mumbling—and in the case of Noreen, blabbing—while our animals shook it up around us. The dogs would seem to improvise a biblical scene about dominance and submission, and they'd corral and chase one another into corners of the field like schoolkids at recess; and we'd analyze their play, and see ourselves in it.

The park felt so idyllic as the summer stretched on and Toby learned about the intensity of thirst and the magic of standing in our long shadows. There he was, sitting in my shade, panting and looking at me. I was a great big tree for him. Amory was like a fairground on Boston's Green Line, with free admission, no dress code, squirrels scampering across picnic tables, nannies with strollers, the scent of pot occasionally tinging the breeze. Only a few blocks from Fenway Park and its game-night thronging and interrogatory lights, its sports fan energy, the game in the distance, Amory carried the eternal air of civilization at its most wistfully mundane.

Sometimes, with the barking, the swirling dog energy, and the heat accelerating our unself-consciousness, I thought we seemed like children at the playground all over again. Forts were built and ponytails tugged—figuratively, but still. It was as close to the unadorned, primitive socializing of *Peanuts* as I've known as an adult. Yes, all of the dynamic problems of groups (read: families) were in the air—the triangular tensions, the unrequited interest, the ganging up, the passive-aggressiveness. But they seemed more in the open air, and not subterranean.

They were as obvious as Toby is when he thinks we can't see he's got a big illicit clump of grass in his mouth.

So parks are for the kids in us, but they're also for kids. At times, that could be a problem. At Amory, dogs and kids, or, more accurately, dogs' parents and kids' parents, were tinder.

The kind of dog person versus antidog person conflict that brought down Winthrop—led by a guy who minded only when dogs, not kids, made noise and tore up grass—was always a threat to Amory. There were screaming matches of all kinds, where somehow it became the kids' rights versus the dogs' rights, a collision of values and philosophies. Not all dog parks in this country are multiuse like those in Brookline, funded for all creatures and not just for dogs to dance around with their wheeling Frisbees and bright rubber balls. Amory was an exercise in coexistence.

The kids sometimes sledded down Amory's snowy hill in the winter, but in the summer they came in full force, like summer people with fold-up chaises in a resort area. They had balloons and baseballs and bats and their own park dreams, and they took over every corner. We loved them; they were kids, and many of us had kids. They played with such commitment, it was transporting in its own way. I watched them with a sweet sense of nostalgia.

But they nonetheless complicated an otherwise relatively controllable dog-park situation. Many of our dogs loved kids, but some didn't. An otherwise-peaceful dog could easily be provoked into growling and baring his teeth by a little person with uncoordinated limbs and loose boundaries stumbling toward him.

And many of the kids loved dogs, but some didn't. There were dogs, especially big dogs, who were so raring to play that they would scare the kids with their enthusiasm, their tails wagging too frenetically, their sniffing noses too close, their barking too abrupt. I remembered that fear, vividly, from when I was a kid. And yet there I was on the other side of the rainbow, wondering how a friendly dog with a panting smile—Toby?—could frighten anyone.

With kids on the scene, dogs and dog owners were suddenly less off-leash, because you had to watch everything so closely, to gauge the rapport and anticipate discord. The sidewalk warriors and sidewalk worriers with kids also liked to spend time at the park during off-leash hours, walking straight into your world or running away from your world terrified—and, in the process, creating stress.

One August morning, a nine- or ten-year-old blond girl—she looked like Renoir's *Girl with a Watering Can*—saw Toby at a distance. She was near first base on one of the unused baseball diamonds, and Toby was sniffing attentively at the rubber home plate, where other dogs had undoubtedly made their mark. He hadn't even noticed her, he was so entranced by what he smelled; but she immediately began to freak out. I could see her, many feet from us on the field, looking as if her mother were trying to lead her into a big bad bear's cage. She was sobbing and so petrified, it seemed like hysteria—like a Beatles concert circa 1964.

Her mother looked at me and said loudly, "I don't know what it is. She's just afraid of dogs."

Then she turned to her daughter, who was cowering behind her, body language at its most explicit, and she said, "Sweetie, it's just a dog. Look, he's friendly." Then the mother turned back to me and said, "She's never had a bad experience with a dog. I don't know what it is."

I couldn't bear to see the little blond girl upset—and at Toby; it was so wrong. The tears were pouring down her cheeks, as she peeked from behind her mother at her vision of hell. I made Toby sit, took his paw, and gave him a cookie, trying to charm her and show her he wasn't all anarchy.

"See," I announced, "he's a good boy. His name is Toby!" But she was inconsolable as he chomped happily, paw still in my hand, eyes still trained on mine. I'd had nightmares about dogs as a little boy, so I understood the depth of the terror. But Toby?

Sometimes a kid was comfortable and actively curious, but the parent was jittery. The kid would be smiling with fresh dimples and reaching out toward Toby, and the parent would be jumpy, probably picturing that soft and chubby new arm with red bite marks in it.

I'd seen that panic in my mother's eye, in the face of dogs and their unpredictability. As a dog owner, I felt as though I could see the parent transmitting fear to the child, and I wanted to try to stop the flow, let the child open the parent's eyes. But the protective terror of a parent was hard to break through with a few dog tricks and gentle talk. Why should a parent trust some stranger in the park?

How could that parent know whether or not I was a Charlotte?

We were all sympathetic at those moments of discord, all innocent—the dog owner and the dog seeking pleasure, the freaked-out kid, the worried parent. Only a sadist, I think, would force the situation and try to create a dog-child-parent connection if the parent was anxious or especially if the kid was panicky.

But for everyone to relax, Toby and I would have to uproot

to another part of the park. Toby was the perfect dog for a kid—sometimes Tom and I joked about adopting a child as a special gift for Toby—but if you don't know dogs, you really don't know dogs. I knew this. All dogs, big and small, playful and slothful, are equally scary to the uninitiated. We had to move on.

So it was an uneasy rapport between dog owners and parents, with strong undercurrents. Dog people resented the intrusion and the knowledge that kids always took precedent over dogs.

I'd hear nondog people say things like "She treats that dog like it's her child," as if that was something to be ashamed of, as if "she" was settling for second best.

It began to make me cringe when I'd hear people compare dogs and kids in such a way that dogs automatically were demoted on the hierarchy of cosmic importance. On a few occasions, Marcella, whose haughty attitude flared up on a regular basis, told me she was glad Tom and I didn't have children, because they would be spoiled to death. She'd laughed when she'd said it, and I'd laughed along with her—but at her tone deafness. Loving a dog and treating it with special kindness and loyalty? Guilty as charged.

We got it: Kids are human, dogs aren't, and humans trump animals. The pecking order was loud and clear. But this was our time to play. This was our park, too. We loved our dogs.

After Winthrop, I felt myself becoming an uncharacteristically stubborn defender and protector of dog-park life, getting testy and argumentative with strangers when they gave me and other dog owners a hard time. I felt ready to go Hayley on someone if need be, like the Night of the White Dog, when she barked at Marv, "What, it's not your job to be a human being?" The conflicts inevitably came down to dogs versus kids, but it should have been a conflict of public rights between adults.

There were special moments, though, that were so Hallmark, you forgot all about your cynicism and resentment and just wanted to stand there taking pictures.

Toby saw himself as another kid, as far as I could tell, and he would sometimes fall in with a couple of children who were playing on the field that summer and charm them, doing full-body wags around them with his ball, dropping it and picking it up, urging them to throw it. This blond dog named Toby, he was like a movie dog to them. I'd stand and watch Toby skipping along with a group of kids and I'd melt. I could see him educating the kids about how to play with a dog, schooling them in fetching and chasing and tug-of-war. If there were disapproving or fearful parents nearby, they didn't make themselves known.

Sometimes an innocent little boy would come to say hello to the dogs, feeling his way toward us, his parents behind him. Some parents were hoping to acclimate their kids to dogs— "Ask if it's okay to pet the puppy, sweetie," they'd say, wisely—in anticipation of getting a dog sometime in the future. Then the child would go to pat Toby on the head, and maybe Toby would lick his face—or the crumbs or juice that were around his mouth.

The nose-to-nose between a kid and a dog can be a beautiful thing. When things go right between a kid and a dog, and between the parent and the owner, it's a happy-all-around moment.

Kids and dogs, innocence squared.

Chewy had had her innocence squashed somehow before she'd fallen into Stan's care, and I still hoped to help restore part of it—the part that could take a cookie without fear.

When she'd enter the park, a fluffy whiteness larking far across the lush green field, I'd stealthily take a cookie out of my pocket. As she got close, rolling through the crowd, I'd hold the cookie up in her direction, checking to be sure other dogs weren't paying attention. And she'd stare right at it, observing her fantasy from afar like the pauper watching the prince, drooling, literally, she wanted it so badly. But no, the man behind the cookie might hurt me. I could see her drama play out in her body movements and her facial expressions, the wary side-eye glance and the hungry mouth and the questioning stance. I'd smile in her direction.

Finally, one steamy day in July, Chewy grabbed the cookie softly from me and ran off. I barely saw it, she was away so fast. I realized I'd felt a feather brush my hand, and then the cookie was gone and she was moving on and chewing. It was a sweet secret transaction. I wanted to go after her and pet her and talk in a high voice to let her know I was happy, but I knew better. I knew much better. This would be a gradual progress, from the guarded pose to the looser world of trust.

As she left me, gobbling up the cookie, she had extra prance in her gait. I looked back; Stan had seen the whole thing and he gave me a nod.

A few times later, after she took the cookie from my hand, which was behind my leg, I made a move to rub her chin. She pulled her head away. One step at a time, I needed to remember. Then after a few more times, she took some neck scratching, but only when she was standing facing my back, so that I could only touch her without looking at her. The power of eye contact was too much for her still.

I must have looked bizarre, petting a dog positioned precisely behind me, reaching my arms in back of my body without turning or looking around. I could feel her warm breath on my hand, imagine the positioning of her head toward my palm, but I couldn't see her there. Sometimes, she'd push her lower jaw against my hand as I scratched, a sure sign that she liked what I was offering.

As she took her cookie and danced at my rear, I began to love this dog. She was Chewy chewing, healing. Her relief began to seem palpable. And this was the park—there were other people who were working out the same thing with her. I saw her taking treats from others' backs, and I even got a little jealous. She was making friends.

So I had to have more. I wanted her to look at me and take a cookie from my smiling face. I had to have eye contact. Some of my closest moments with Toby were spent looking in his face, learning his expressions of mouth-open contentment or watching his head nodding as his eyes closed. Sometimes at the park, Toby would steal a look at me in the middle of play with another dog, to make sure I was watching him in his glory. The quiet exchange of regard was one of the richest parts of dog ownership, that sidebar of love.

It progressed incrementally over weeks with Chewy, to the

point where she'd come to see me at the park, face me, full-body-wagging her butt with its white torch of a tail, take the treat as well as the lovin', and make eye contact—a moment of white furry smiling with black lips. And then she'd move on to another lover, only to return a few minutes later for more from me. Within months, we'd achieved communal victory, one cookie and one blink at a time.

She was at home. The courtship had worked.

families of choice

That summer, I noticed settling cracks in the stucco on the mansions that stood on a hill over the west side of the park, where the sun went down through sky-bound oak branches. I found myself staring in that direction a lot in the evenings.

Those Amory sunsets triggered a basic human response to beauty, a horizon painting of blue becoming purple, with an orange dot about to melt behind a roof. While their dogs played, people always took note of the western sky as the colors sank and sneaked through the buildings of the city. Renoir.

Bertha was the dog who'd been most maternal to Toby, an older female who'd taken him under her wing. I continued to enjoy the way she'd march over, reddish hair shimmying, and take a stick from him just because she could; and he'd give it right up, aware of her superiority. It was comic, their little routine. She was quietly schooling him during his first year, a friend and big sister.

We humans talk about families of choice—among gay people, long-term friends, stepfamilies, untraditional people. Dogs have been all over that idea forever; they take on a new familial position with each pack they breeze through—with other dogs, and with humans. Bertha was Toby's favorite sibling for many, many good days in the sun and in the rain.

Some afternoons, Nash would say to me, apropos of nothing, "I'm having an 'I love Bertha' day. I'm just so into her today." He'd look down at her as she sat panting and looking gorgeous, Grace Kelly. And hers was a true beauty; whenever someone mentioned Bertha in conversation, anyone who knew her said, "Aw, Bertha."

She was the ideal of a golden retriever—not the breed standard, perhaps, but the tops in temperament. She was the dog who'd lean against you and you'd scratch and massage her neck and pat her head, and when you stopped, she'd kick her cold nose and snout under your hand—just once—and then, if you didn't continue, run off to another lover. She was a lover.

I knew the "I love you" feeling Nash would have with Bertha—those sweet days when Toby stole my heart thirty times instead of twenty, when my dog became my best friend more than he was my charge. At my desk, I'd sit looking at the little putz king, enjoying very sweet eye contact. Sometimes, while I was lying on the couch to watch something on TV for work, Toby would climb up, put his body between my legs, rest his head on my belly, and stare at me as he nodded off. He looked so trusting and so safe.

My exchange for the love he brought to my life was time at the park. Those moments when Toby was drowsy after an hour or two of play were particularly divine. Bertha was a more peaceful, sedentary dog than Toby, frequently in the down position, a look of mild contentment on her face. But she loved the park, too, where she was among her kind—other dogs as well as humans with hands that could pet her—and where she could snack on some fresh grass. Nash had his high-strung moments, his humor less prone to settling on the ground; Bertha brought him there. That was their park caravan.

When Bertha got sick, it seemed to come out of nowhere. Another dog, so soon after Chester? At least with Chester, there had been a history of medical issues. Bertha was still young. One day, Nash said he thought she looked lethargic, and she was coughing softly. That night, she refused dinner, the most basic of bad signs. Even hamburger didn't appeal. And so Nash and Bette took her to Angell, the nearby animal hospital. The diagnosis was dire, Nash said in an e-mail late that night. Cancer all over the place, fluid around the heart, no hope. She was going. Sometimes e-mail is so cold and final.

And there it was, the last act foreshadowed, the big flashforward to the near future: shaved fur, exhaustion, coughing, and week and weeks of farewell. I could see it coming, but I didn't want to waste the time between then and now. I was not going to walk away from Bertha while I could still see her.

Godsend: Right after Bertha's diagnosis, Nash and Bette were going away, and Nash asked me if Tom and I would be willing to take Bertha for a weekend.

"Uh, yuh."

It was a fantasy come true. In the period between the diagnosis and the inevitable, Nash was giving Toby a weekend with Bertha all to himself. And with Tom and me, too. I can't help but think that Toby and Bertha knew the end was approaching. That was my human estimation, the projection I'd chosen to believe. I knew it was tenuous, but I liked the idea. But if they really did know, if they smelled sickness, as some say dogs do, then they didn't show it. Maybe they were saying good-bye and it was emotion-free, just a nod to say "See ya there."

We loved that girl up all weekend, with constant treats and petting. And we felt lucky, too, that our dog still had a long journey ahead of him. We got Toby and Bertha up on the bed with us and pushed toys in their faces and left kisses on their soft heads. Tom was glad that my trips to the park, this life I'd established without him, had yielded Bertha—he was a golden retriever guy, with memories of his golden, Teddy, still on the tip of his tongue. And he was glad about Nash and about Margo when he met them. He was beginning to get used to my park stories. "So write a book," he'd say, laughing at me.

Bertha was a little breathless that weekend, parts of her body were shaved, and there were meds to administer, but she was still able to climb onto and off of our bed. We stared at her as she slept in the morning on the bedspread in the space between our bodies, and she stared back at us when she woke—until Toby broke through our sight lines to make sure we weren't forgetting about him.

It was a gift to have two days of intense focus on a dog we'd probably see only a few more times, and then among groups of people and dogs. It was intimate and bittersweet. Good-bye, Bertha.

———

At the end of August, a week or two before she died, Nash was trying to leave the park to go home and work. He'd said good-bye to the people and was trying to lead Bertha up to Amory Street, as always. But Bertha, looking steadily ahead, was all about staying. She was definitely still strong enough to walk the few blocks home, but she'd decided to stay, that command that we teach them so well: Stay.

Nash pulled at the leash, laughing but intent. "Come on, you." He was standing over her in his shorts and baseball cap, trying to move on.

And Bertha slunk down even more with all her eighty pounds of orange redness, looking up at Nash from the grass with pure insolence and playfulness.

"I'm going to stay right here in the park," she seemed to say, "I'm on strike." Her voice, as Nash had performed it, was high and a little wanton. (He talked to her all day long, and she talked back to him, too. I knew that.) "No," she insisted a little huffily, "I want to stay here."

She may have even taken a quick bite of grass and dirt to show her commitment to rebellion. Nash dropped the leash and laughed. Bertha wins. "She wins!" he exclaimed, a last burst of public love for her.

That year, Nash had seen his kids move on, one to college and the other to a postcollege journey of career and love. They were his finest creations. But in his daily life, in the moment-to-moment existence, now there was this imminent death. We usually get a lifetime with our kids, but only years with our dogs. Bertha would be leaving soon, and so, eventually, would Travis, and Stewie, and Trixie, and Zelda, in a long succession of great friends. Toby, too. This was the natural way of life on

Earth, so sad but not tragic, the good-bye to a beloved dog; but still it held tight.

When the dog you treasured was dying, you felt immense, classic sorrow. I saw it with Drew, and now I could see it with Nash. Loss, not just the anticipation of loss, or the remembrance of it. All love and loss.

"I'll be staying here," Bertha said that day at Amory, plunked down on the ground, unmovable, like tree roots. It was a photo, a part of that album in your heart of true loves: Bertha playing in the park.

And so I'd gotten it. There was the why. It had emerged from the snow, like the bright R. Crumb cigar. As the seasons passed, I had begun to understand and accept the bargain. Why get a dog when its life will end, probably before yours? Because it's worth the pain of loss. A year in, I could see clearer than ever that all the clichés were true. Once you loved a dog, once you knew the depth of love you could have for an animal, once you loved a dog while understanding that he or she would probably leave before you, you were a richer person for the rest of your life. Once you let them in, they were in. They were part of your eternity. You were now the sole living member of the caravan you formed together, but the caravan went on.

And there is something life-changing and essential about being animals together, in the moment, with your dog. Dogs, especially in park scenarios, remind us that we also have naked desires underneath our defenses and our protective layers, that we, too, are creatures who live in packs and who need to play. There will be blood, and fights, and humping, and premature losses, but there will be moments of joy among dogs that seem to come straight from our human DNA. With so many screens in our lives, a dog is a nonclickable link to nature that is profound. The simple and direct responses of a dog, the tail wagging and the smiles and the growls and the chasing and the ball love, they are sweet and profound and corrective for us when life is alienating.

For me, Toby had become what poet Jane Kenyon called her dog in the poem "After an Illness, Walking the Dog"—he was "the designated optimist" in my life. I looked at him and remembered that there was nothing more important on my schedule than play with others—at the park, yes, and also when I was working, or socializing, or just walking alone along the Charles River. Control, finality, fear, they all faded away in the ready eyes of my dog.

Of course Toby would leave Tom and me someday, and perhaps we'd leave his toys on that picnic table, unlabeled. But I was blocking the fact as much as I could, successfully, rather than obsessing about his death so much that I forgot to enjoy him. I was not pregrieving him, just savoring him. What Jimmy Stewart said about Grace Kelly at her funeral was also true of her dog double, Bertha, and will always be true of Toby, too: "Grace brought into my life as she brought into yours, a soft, warm light every time I saw her, and every time I saw her was a holiday of its own." When your dog dies, you have that holiday permanently stored in your heart, that regular reminder of warm light. You have that warm light.

After that first fall and winter with Toby, after I stopped holding him back with the leash when we arrived at Amory, I began to let him draw me out of my refined depression and into a more unedited life, where people meet by chance; he pulled me across the bridge. More life. I tried to stop holding myself back so hard out of fear of losing; I tried not to pre-grieve. He was playing out his half of the "boy and his dog" vision, but with an instinctive awareness that both this particular boy and this particular dog needed to let go, socialize more hazardously. Toby, still so young, had no wish to live in a bubble with me.

Toby had made me a more contented, freer person, someone who lives and loves despite the outcome, someone who risks play and who no longer needs to forge excuses. When I can't hear his panting, furry blond head nearby, and feel the weight of him on my feet, and smell his paws, and feel his confidence and cheerfulness and automatic forgiveness, I will still have his spirit embedded in mine. He will exert his presence; he will be a part of my everlasting family of choice. That little goose I unhooked at the park every day—I will remember how he took me into his caravan, how he pushed me to play ball, how he led me onto the field, how he let me off the leash.

outro

One winter afternoon, Toby ran into my office and threw down a groundhog toy. At five months, he was a pint-size ball of willpower. He wanted to go to the park, right then, it was clear. Tom wasn't going to take him; they had their own thing on the sidewalks. Tom had let Toby and me find our way through the park world without him, and I was happy to see Toby and Tom find their way along the cracks in the sidewalk. Their caravan had them sniffing together as a pair, walking in peace.

Toby was still a little stuffed animal–shaped guy, just beginning to know what he liked. He picked up and threw down the toy a second time, then looked up at me, waiting. A soft but clear statement. Now.

And, reader, I couldn't wait to oblige.

To go out with Toby on a trek to the park sounded just about right. We rushed down the stairs of the apartment building, a jumble of feet and paws and legs, and set off, his head out the back window of the car, my eyes watching him smile in my side mirror. His snout was pointed up, sniffing what was happening, loving it. And I, too, was sniffing away.

And then there we were at the gate of Amory, and for a second I felt I should make him sit. The faint urge remained. That was what trainer Don had said to do, and that was what seemed civilized. But it was completely silly today to hold any living thing back for a single second from happiness and dance. I unhooked Toby, didn't bother with the quash moment anymore. Let go of it. Then put the leash in the pocket and just kept following.

glossary

To bungee out: You can always extricate yourself from unwanted park conversation by suddenly becoming very, very interested in your dog. "Oops, he's about to poop," you might say before making your escape.

The caravan effect: It's the poetic justice of dog ownership that your dog confirms your view of the world or directly challenges it, thereby becoming your fateful partner in the progress of your identity. At the park, you and your dog are a little caravan of personality together. In a visual equivalent of the caravan effect, you also look like your dog, or you don't look like your dog at all. The two of you are an optical full rhyme or a nonrhyme, inescapably related across a stanza.

The Charlottes: They're at every dog park, owners unwilling to take responsibility for their dogs' aggression, no matter how many exasperated people confront them. A Charlotte is always able to dissect a violent dogfight in such a way as to prove that her dog is innocent. Other owners must watch out as a Charlotte and her dog walk the park like an incipient storm system.

The clear bag phenomenon: Some owners stand holding clear bags of poop, and you can spy greenish brown logs through the steamed-up plastic. It's TMVI: too much visual information.

Dam burstage: This happens when someone makes an unexpected confession to an anonymous dog person at the park. Sometimes it's easier to tell all to a stranger in the presence of animals who'll love you no matter what.

Dog ventriloquism: If you want to say something to someone near you at the park, you can say it through your dog. Your dog can serve as your dummy, as if you are a child putting words in the mouth of a doll.

Humpdar: It's like gaydar, which is when you can detect a gay affiliation. You can quickly sense your dog's desire to hump, see the sparkle in his or her eye the moment he or she spots the right dog entering the pack.

Overthanking: This happens when a vigilant person yells, "Yoo-hoo, your dog pooped," and you thank them with a little too much good cheer. Your words express appreciation, but your thought balloon reads "Yoo-hoo, stop interrupting me." It's a shot of gratitude with a hint of bitter.

Pack of freaks: This describes what the park people might seem like when you first go to the park with your dog, and what the dog-park community ultimately is. The atmosphere of spontaneous dog play, dogfights, humping, and anonymity can inspire unusual behavior in owners.

Poop mime: You do it after your dog poops, when others are watching you. "See," says your thought balloon as you very conspicuously hold your bag and bend over, moving like a silent-film star, "I'm a good citizen."

Poop delinquents: Every park has owners who ignore their dogs as they wander in search of their poop spot. These poop delinquents chat away, forgetting their dogs' most basic purpose. They're negligent, often flaky, sometimes quite nice, and, alas, they never learn.

Poop rebels: These poop delinquents are more offensive, as they willfully refuse to pick up their dogs' poop. They're not spacey or distracted; they're just brazen repudiators. Whether from narcissism or despair, entitlement or contempt, they seem to reject the fact that they live in a world with other people.

Sidewalk warriors: These are the walkers who refuse to veer from their path when they spot an owner and an on-leash dog ahead. They aggress as they progress. One reason to go to the park.

Sidewalk worriers: These are the walkers who veer off in a big, big way when they spot an owner and an on-leash dog ahead. Overly fearful, they make you feel like a pair of monsters. Yet another reason to go to the park.

To poop it forward: When you happen upon a stray bowel movement and pick it up, you are an especially Good Samaritan. You are investing in your karma. Bagging your own baby's fresh poop is easy, but grabbing the cold, weighty, crusty artifact of a mysterious dog is gagworthy.

acknowledgments

There are people without whom I wouldn't have written this book. Mary Bachmann and Chris Sproat fed me heaps of food and friendship and love for many, many months. They were always up for it. Lee Glickenhaus was the listener we all deserve, also for many months. Joan McNaught took me to another level of thought and understanding. David Gilbert kept me real; always does.

And Tom McNaught is the husband of husbands, the guy this is all for, my guy.

My mother, Miriam London, is still young and lovely. Now able to be in the same room as Toby and tell me how beautiful he is, she gets special thanks. So does my friend who is also a cousin, Jeff Mickelson. He is as loyal as a dog, and I know I would be lost without him. My sustaining lifelong friend Tom Davey gave wise, sympathetic counsel, as always. Ellen Sugarman is a bunch of laughs; I get her.

Joan Anderman gave me her ever-inspiring camaraderie—oh, and an agent, too. Ellen Geiger has been my astute, honest, and generous bridge to the publishing industry. She quickly became a friend. And that publishing industry as embodied by my astute editors Pete Wolverton, Anne Brewer, and Mary Willems has been a happy breeze. Caroline Leavitt, Randy Susan Meyers, Maureen Dezell, David Wiegand, you gave strong advice and helped me make choices. The writing was assisted by visits from Ben Mickelson, walks with Bill Engel, and phone calls with Louise Herman. Sarah Rodman was invaluable—honest reader, friend, colleague.

Thanks go to everyone at Amory, now and then and tomorrow, for tolerating this intrusion. Among them, so many friends: Joan Rachlin, Gilson and Luciana Schachnik, Steve Shatkin, Linda Baron, Paul Sibelle and Julie Chao-Sibelle, Victoria Moskowitz, Denny Kanarek, Ben Isaacson, Kathy Kelety, Dan Wolfson, Andrea Testa, Laurie Jannelli, Rich Schmid, C.J. Lori, Robert Volk, Kevin Lehrer, Kate Patterson, Mark Penzel, Cathy Corman, Val Maas, Julie Sher, Will and Nisa Dailey, Thom Kidrin, Chloe Comins, Chad Barraford, Joel, Ronna, Claudia, Phil and Jessica, Lenny and Stephanie, Eamon and Emerald, Bob and Angela, Aaron and Ann. Lance Mulleneaux, you were Nooner's great big guy.

There have been other good friends at the park, too: Rosie, Jesse, Roxy, Miles, Daisy, Alexis, Sydney, Hank, Chula, Buddy, Moose, Ella, Mona, Pele, Millie, Maeby, Bradlee, Pogey, Lefty, Lucy, Mingus, Maggie, Maggie, Maggie, and Maggy. Too many to name, none of them forgotten.

A number of *Boston Globe* friends make work fly—Mark Shanahan, Geoff Edgers, Katie Johnston, that's you. Meredith Goldstein gave me tons of advice and friendship. Don Aucoin is a great, loyal, and informative buddy—he would say "pal"—there from the start. Everyone deserves a Don. Devra First and my other beloved Support Ho's were a tight, secure net. Doug Most, Marty Baron, Rebecca Ostriker, and Michael Brodeur are the kind editors who generously let me go for a few months without a guilt complex. They have my respect and thanks, and so do my current Globe editors, Brian McGrory, Janice Page, and Hans Schulz. Hayley Kaufman ushered my early thoughts about Amory into the pages of the Globe, and the "G" copy desk, as always, kept me safe. I still open gifts every day from past Globies Scott Powers, Mary Jane Wilkinson, Scott Heller, Kevin Kelly, Lincoln Millstein, John Ferguson, and many others.

I feel deep appreciation and affection for the *Globe* readers who've indulged me all these years. You've made my job rewarding, a vibrant conversation that will go on, I hope.

Oh, and Toby, thanks for the long conversations, too. You're a goose.